Redwood Writers
2019 Poetry Anthology

Crow

In the Light of Day,
In the Dark of Night

Les Bernstein and Fran Claggett-Holland
Co-editors

Susan Gunter, Louise Hofmeister and Belinda Riehl
Editorial Assistants

Linda L. Reid
Board Liaison

An anthology of poetry
by Redwood Writers
A branch of the
California Writers Club

Redwood Writers 2019 Poetry Anthology:
Crow
In the Light of Day, In the Dark of Night

Editors
Les Bernstein and Fran Claggett-Holland

ISBN: 978-0-9977544-5-2

Book design
by Jo-Anne Rosen
Wordrunner Publishing Services

Cover art
by Christine MacDonald

Interior art
by Warren Bellows

Published by Redwood Writers Press
PO Box 4687
Santa Rosa, California 95402

something to crow about...

in the present tense
it stirs and wakes
a concentrated industry
called onward by spirits
provoked by happenstance
overseen by muses
and indisputably alive

in this new unsettled territory
with its gravitational pull
we grope for direction
or bone marrow certainty
in a seeming white page void

did we capture the enormous once
or will it land with a plunk
will it percolate with sneaky tenderness
or just be a deviation of familiar
will it spark knowing nods
or be noise and future dust

there is no simple formula
to resonate and transfuse
you were brave
you put it down
you sent it in
here it is
you are among friends

— Les Bernstein

Contents

In the Light of Day, In the Dark of Night

CROW

The Bird and Our Artists

In the Light of Day, In the Dark of Night

The crow is an amazing bird, rich in mythology and ritual, a frequent subject for artists and poets. It is also a bird studied widely by scientists, who assess its brain as equal to that of a seven year old child; it is capable not only of using tools, but of fashioning them to attain a particular object. It has elaborate family rituals, gathering for funerals of one of its dead. It forms attachments to humans, recognizing them by face, and often rewards their kindnesses by bestowing shiny trinkets where there once was food. A recent Facebook video even showed a crow giving a piece of bread to a mouse which had initially scurried away from the crow with its treasure.

The editors are more than pleased to have two artists celebrating *CROW, In the Light of Day, In the Dark of Night,* Redwood Writers 2019 poetry anthology: Christine MacDonald and Warren Bellows, our longtime friend and contributor of two previous covers. The editors both immediately chose Warren Bellows' evocative crow, showing all its mysterious powers as it flies through a shadowy world with an intent clear to the viewer. This crow, done in black and grey, takes us into the poems of the five Award of Merit winners. One of Warren Bellows' poems, "found" on his easel, gives us insight into how this talented artist goes about his work:

Notes on My Easel

1. Be willing to lose the familiar
2. When you are lost, stay authentic with the next step
3. Trust the "God Gestures" when they come
4. Keep still...even for a long time if necessary
5. Simplify the composition
6. Remember that all mistakes are openings

7. Talk to your painting
8. Listen to what it says
9. Dance when you feel stuck
10. Keep exploring the mystery of grays

The paintings of Christine MacDonald, which have given us the front and back covers of the book, hold their mystery close while conveying emotions close to the heart. The artist describes her work for us this way:

Christine MacDonald's paintings often depict evocative encounters between wild creatures, or, between humans and creatures. She is particularly drawn to using images of ravens, crows and hares in her work. These creatures inhabited the landscapes of her childhood, growing up on the remote Hebridean island of Tiree, off the west coast of Scotland. The realization that they all share the distinction of being mythologized as otherworldly presences worldwide, and not only in Celtic folklore, came later.

Christine studied fine art at the University of Sussex, England, and graduated with a B.A. degree with honors, in painting. She maintains a studio near the town of Sonoma, where ravens and jackrabbits still share the land. Her sense of reverence for, and longing for, a wordless communication with nature (the Other) drives her work—sometimes poignantly, sometimes with humor.

We are honored to showcase these two Sonoma artists in our anthology.

We extend our thanks to Redwood Writer volunteer proofreaders: Susan Gunter, Louise Hofmeister and Belinda Riehl. Our book design genius Jo-Anne Rosen, our meticulous webmaster Joelle Burnett, and our go-to-for-all questions Linda Loveland Reid have made this book possible. Our thanks to them and to the Redwood Writers Board of Directors for supporting this project.

— *Fran Claggett-Holland*

Redwood Writers
Award of Merit Poets

Margaret Barkley

Briahn Kelly-Brennan

Patricia Nelson

Florentia Scott

Jo Ann Smith

Dust Bin

There they are —
sweepings from another day
haircut clippings
used prayers
chips of broken glass and your mother's
best Spode china
police reports
mild regrets
and wrenching grief

When you cut your losses and walk away,
what falls to the floor?
There is no rug to sweep it under
no way to leave it behind,
like we'd hoped

Like a wake behind us
like clattering cans tied to the honeymoon car,
we move ahead, and our discards follow,
sulking, glittering

until one day
we sigh,
tired of our own incessant striving
and turn to face
what has become
a glorious vanguard
behind us, proclaiming
Yes, we have lived

Junkyard Dog

Let's say, for the sake of discussion,
that before you were born you were made of light,
or something like it.
Let's say that you were not *anything* at all
like this oddly shaped living thing
(no offense)
that you are now,

but that something of you existed.
Maybe you were just more see-through
or more vast, or fluffier,
but there you were
then in one excited wet moment
the body you know
began, grew for nine months, and landed here.

It was the luck of the draw exactly where—
probably not onto towels on a dirt floor, for example.
My guess is that you arrived in a well-lit sterile room,
probably naked for just a second,
and then you began collecting things,
because that's what we do.

And now here you are —
here we are together in these bodies,
living in a culture *filled* with things,
in a country where the people in charge
are like dumb
drooling junkyard dogs,
protecting their piles of metal and drums of oil,
even sending some of us
to faraway places to do their bullying for them.

We don't know how to be with this
but do the best we can,
collecting things — food, clothes and houses
electronic devices and to-do lists,
earning money to collect more things, and
trying to have a good time in the process.

Meanwhile,
we start to feel a wee bit protective,
like junkyard dogs ourselves, even,
guarding the piles of stuff that we've gathered,
taking things a little too personally sometimes

and lunging at the fence
we've built around all of it.
It's all so much that sometimes
we have to hire insurance people
and attorneys to help.

But here's the great thing —
in the middle of all of this
collecting and protecting
we seem to have been granted,
most of the time,
the ability to learn
and to feel

and to notice what was here all along,
like sunsets
wild-ass fields of orange poppies
and the fact that having a body
is actually quite wonderful
especially when we're
rubbing them around on each other,
or dancing.

We discover that loving someone else
feels better than anything,
and that the important stuff
can't be collected at all.

Somewhere along the way,
there is that tin man moment,
when you know you have a heart
because it's breaking

and you realize that courage is nothing
like a slavering fanged dog —
courage is being willing to let go,
open the damn gate
and share the goods.

If you're lucky,
by the time you're old you've found humility,
which doesn't mean that you're unimportant,
it means that you're *everything* —
because we're all made out of the same stuff,
some kind of light,
something vast and fluffy
covered in skin.

Her Time

She was born
under the belly of the sun,

which explains a few things.

She was born at that time
when the tilt of the planet
makes us all lean away from the light,

when, whether we like it or not,
the quiet voice of darkness calls us in.

She was born when the trees are bare in the cold,
and anything alive is hiding,
or should be.

She doesn't mind waiting,
like the winter fox with taut muscles
at the edge of a rabbit's hole,

or the bear,
curled up in the dark, slowed
almost to death.

She is not afraid of the hidden things.
She reaches into the deep folds of darkness
lets its skeletal hand point the way for her.

She knows the dances of bone and earth,
the crystalline visions that come from eyes
grown used to the night.

She carries this all year long,
but this is the time
when we must go with her.

She knows the way.
This is her time.

Ribs

Flying down the road to town
my mind already there,
I slow suddenly,
shocked into the present
by a perfect set of ribs
jutting up in the middle of my lane
gleaming wet and red in the morning sun
with the tan fur of the body
splayed out flat beneath.

A young deer,
must have been hit in the night.
Already picked by vultures,
this red cage so exposed
I can't turn away
and in that sunlit vision
of small bones
I feel my own ribs picked clean,

my own heart beating
inside its cage
as wet and red as this —
bones arrayed as fingers
of two skeletal hands cupped
to hold precious the center muscle
so loyal to me,
driving blood a thousand miles
through my body.

In one drive-by moment
I am the same as any bony mammal,
the same as you —
fragile and moist,
flesh and blood and breath
held by bone
held by some grace we cannot see
held by time given
till bone exposed again.

Secret Pleasures

Spring is pouring over everything
Unrepentant,
wearing colors much too bright
for any other kind of party

Everywhere you look
there are show-offs —

The cow nudging her still-wet calf to walk
unsteadily in a field of bright yellow
mustard

Red-winged blackbirds swooping and
looping from fence post to tree

Hills vivid and extravagant in green
Horses belly deep in grass

And the light itself somehow brighter,
unfiltered, unabashed

The smells of flowers and green shoots and new
air all competing
blending
inside of me
enough to make me moan

If you listen you will hear
the heavy breathing of the earth
herself —
beads of dampness have collected
on her huge inner thighs,
opened

Her sap has risen
And mine
And yours

Spring has spilled over everything

In towns you will see it too —
New skin is everywhere
Breasts are blooming
People smiling with secret pleasures
are tempted to share them with you

Crow

For Fran

maybe it's not that hard, Crow
maybe I can just say
I am afraid
(bow twice, present to us
the shiny objects of your discernments
that we dazzle into verse at your enthrall)

the pull of your mate
already gone, thin as air
across your wings
(you circle, feather, and spread
tuck a little something
into each opening mind)

her meaning in your world
ruffles memories
like a voice
(we hold you with the small warm strings
of our poems)

too soon will come the day
when these anchors
are no match
for the wind

How to Plant Seed Without Dreaming of Summer Tomatoes

I climbed a mountain once
More than once
More than one
To see the world differently

More than once
Eased down into thickening air
From seeing the world differently
And began to forget

Easing down into thick air
Moment by moment
I began to forget
I had to forget

To live one moment
Not more than one
I must forget
I climbed a mountain once

Ice

Today comes up cold
Melts blue
All over the afternoon
Where white bears walk
On hard hard water

Consumed

Desire as big as the valley
When flat orange light hounds the horizon
In the reckless shadows of coyote brush
Through the timid clatter of reed grass
Among manzanita's hasty leaves
Here here here and now

The purring of untamed teeth
When flat orange light hounds the horizon
Through the timid clatter of reed grass
An endless feral seeking

A soft bit of grey or brown
In the reckless shadows of coyote brush
Among manzanita's hasty leaves
Behind between beneath

Desire as big as the valley
Here here here and now
The purring of untamed teeth
An endless feral seeking
A soft bit of grey or brown
Behind between beneath

Briahn Kelly-Brennan

Mice at Night

The windy night is swinging light
All along the hall
The wood stove's bright to fight cold's bite
Outlines stalk the wall

The cat becomes a lion
The mouse is two feet tall

The door squeaks high when mice sneak by
Low in the glow of the flame
In the line of sight, if the timing's right
The hunger among us seeks prey

And the fire begins to roar
As the lion walks away

Night in Purgatory

Night means something here
where the dead reoccur
between a mountain and a starred sky.

Where stars mark the end of Hell,
with a higher burning: lit and angled stones.
Where all on the slope look crookedly.

They go lopsided up the mountain,
on a memory of eye and heel,
breathe a strange air bent by meaning.

They must stop sharply in the pointed night,
the dark that touches them like thorns.
Must accustom themselves to the heaviness of stars,

To the footing unlike climbing,
and the different rising of dream, apart
from the jointed metaphor of the body.

They remember their time on earth
where, deep in its color of leather,
their brown eyes searched the rocks,

Foretelling the small, dry branches,
usual in that latitude
and loud in the wind as sparrows.

The mind remembers the tall planets,
their colors covered with a language of
light and distance and flying not spoken in Florence.

The eye remembers being lost, a marsh
overtaken by the strange blue lights and the damp,
the soft muds and their varicose paths.

They remember and go on, barter the grey rocks
of their errors for the difficult, empty circles of sight:
Atonement they will carry toward the stars.

Star

—a tarot card

See the stars in the daylight sky,
everywhere the points of shine.
Bent at a shape of water

is a woman with star-colored hair.
In the light of yellow and white
she has no shadow. She gathers air

and water with her bowls' bright rings.
Her foot rests on the river without weight or sinking.
Around her, starlight moves and pours.

It matters like the water in her hands.
And it seems that she has always been here,
in someone's dream of innocence.

She and the dreamer
breathe the colors of her window,
the light already and always open.

In some dark elsewhere lies the sweating mine,
the war. She will never see them
and the dreamer wants it so.

In this window, only the odd clarity:
star and water, dazzle of yellow flower,
the little scarlet bird alive in its edges.

Narcissus

I cannot look at you — or anyone.
My sister is dead, who wore my face.
The gods who loved me are angry.

The cornice of my days has fallen,
the light and dark go everywhere,
the colors sideways like winds.

The sky is loud in its waves, the blue gone.
But my face floats in the small pond
where my eyes are upward.

I don't see beauty there, but nearness to the dark.
I see its rocking outline bleed or breathe,
its exhalation of black birds.

My stillness is a cave where some darks move
like ferns, and some are deep and sharp as reefs.
And there is only one clear face as silent as a light.

Siren Searching

The ball of light is in my eye again
grows full and rattles like a dial.
I tap with a foot the white and quiet rock,
the loud, black sea, this swirl of time.

I am a vertigo of shine and shadow
long among the sounds alive as wolves.
I am dark at the edge and wasting
for one brighter and more beautiful than I.

Will I find him or die searching still?
Will I love as I dream the floating images —
invading again with my ear against the circles,
the red, receding hooves of the sun.

I who lean always toward the listener,
my feet singing as I dance.
They turn like moons, they are white,
they burn in the whirling light.

Around me floats my sound, repeating,
a beat like a gambler slapping down
a lamp-lit sum of number and a color,
and that strange echo that is beauty.

In my hands, dark will tilt and wail upward,
eat the glowing air from everywhere,
hurl light, a storm of snow and birds. I die
of my lengthening hands and their sky full of song.

Believer's Candle

Believer, make a candle.
Make it crude and bright as you,
short and thick and beating like a hoof.

The world needs dark about it
to make it stay and mean, and
loud, round lights to hold like badges.

So lift the lights that burn,
love the moths that drop
and shake black noise against the skin.

Believer, come scalded with a death, expulsion.
Come starved to water and your wish for water.
Come all the way to a sad and knowing wish to continue.

Love this believer in his failing wax,
his world that softens and deceives
if you hold to it a light too gentle or too long.

Builder

Jack builds boats
from toilet paper rolls and bubble wrap,
broken necklace string,
packing paper and oddly-shaped box lids.
With tape and glue
and fragments of information
gleaned from classroom lessons, cartoons,
bits of conversation dropped
by careless adults holding wineglasses and finger food,
and a universe of knowledge
unfolding like a baby bird
within his growing mind.

Clouds and light ever changing

Clouds and light ever changing
hide the mountains that move as the clouds but more slowly.
From here the forest is a smooth dappled green,
dark as hearts,
but the paths are blocked by fallen trees.
It is difficult to walk
and we thought we would have to go back
without completing our journey.
I try to feel awe
but mountains no longer move me.
Just a song
an expression
just a yearning
unsuppressed as mine
shared as mine is not.
Human faces, human voices
call.
I see only mountains and clouds growing darker
and rain.

Inside outside

In the forest beyond the city, scents gather:
damp earth, sun-warmed pine needles,
trampled grass, ceanothus, stagnant water.

And unwashed human hair.

That was unexpected. It is but does not belong.

I stop, I turn, I sniff, but it is gone.

Like a thought
that appears and disappears,
disturbing but soon forgotten.

Like a shadow along the floor,
a tail vanishing around a corner,
that you know you saw but might have imagined.

Like a familiar phrase rearranged by software,
into something comical or nonsensical but in a way, deeply profound,
a reordering of the world along different principles, sudden chaos.

And through the chaos bursts an insight
of something that was there all along but never noticed,
an expanse of blue water
unseen behind the screen of brush that now,
transformed to a layer of ashes,
no longer blocks the view.

Familiar but unknown.
There but not there.
Living but no longer among us.
What is but never was.

Landscape, imagined

Clouds pouring down between two mountain peaks
might cloak the movements of gods and heroes
or of men who cut trees in the forest,
where dampness pearls on coat collars
and boots scrape sodden moss off rocks.

Through tunnels of ever-lightening blue
through the islands and along the mainland shore
does the sea wind around that farthest headland
and continue on into forever
to unknown lands with magical beings?

Or does it end at a fog-enshrouded dock
where paint peels off buildings
and unshaven men in baseball caps,
with yellowed teeth and unquiet eyes
pinch cigarette butts with darkened fingers?

Sunset kiss

We sit on the beach, watching the earth turn away from the light,

seeing the hueless air transform to something a dreamer might
imagine

a dream of red and purple, orange, gold, blue and pure blinding white

until the horizon flashes green and flattens, dark against the pale
yellow sky.

We sit on this barkless tree uprooted long ago,

flayed, made smooth in its evolution towards sawdust swirling on
the sea bottom.

Your arm is warm around my waist, your cheek scrapes mine,

but your lips are soft and your mouth is moist and warm.

Your eyes are blue in the turning light, then storm-sea green, now
darkening amber.

Your eyes open as you kiss, onto starlight and moon upon the water.

The warmth of your body flowing into mine is here.

Your hands moving across me are now.

And we won't ask the ending, though we know all stories end.

We are now,

transforming.

Were They Singing

*(written after the Pittsburgh massacre
in the synagogue)*

were they
singing, praying, daydreaming
was the Rabbi droning on
maybe they were sleeping
I used to fall asleep in church

the embrace of sabbath peace
brought them to the shul that day
where unsuspected terror struck

senseless serial assaults
spike my blood pressure
even evoke a momentary outrage
then fade
often before the next news cycle begins

this one
threatens my balance
spinning dizzy
falling on my knees immobile
stuck in centuries old tear-soaked mud
not ready to resurrect

what is this sorrow
I am not a Jew
what is this compulsion to
tightly hold this pain
as if letting go would shatter a trust
but with whom

tomorrow
time
the grand arbiter
may work its magic
begin to crowd out
yesterday's biddings

but today
aware the sound of breaking glass
has never cost me more than
just an inconvenience
today
eighty years since Kristallnacht
today I am a Jew

Jo Ann Smith

The Bearded Man's Wife

Large terre de faience pitcher
by Picasso

If I gazed at your face five hundred times,
I might not see the mystery there
behind your blank expressionless stare,
or would I?

the brushed irregular glaze
of your face, stained perhaps by tears,
like the one about to fall from your eye,
bears no resemblance
to your more vivid mate,
the eponymous Bearded Man,
his masculine face a rich smooth bronze,
expressive, decidedly dominant

your hair hangs loosely on the left
tightly braided on the right
held back with adorning
ribbons and bows, a whimsical leaning?
yet how to know your nature
whether carefree or contained

who were you
why is your face
frozen in anonymity
were you a woman of substance, a vessel of life
more than the "Bearded Man's Wife"?

the multidimensional ewer of you
the curves and dips and depths
of the white earthen clay
reveal as a flat, plain mask.
your eyes, if not frightened, lack passion
as if they see nothing
as if you were to yourself invisible

I could see your face five hundred times more
to explore what Picasso ignored.
a plainly exposed misogynist
he captured your beauty, it was all that he saw.
whether lapse or intention
your dimension was sadly dismissed;
you should have been painted with awe.

Jo Ann Smith

Again

persimmons are coming again
the wind is holding its breath
waiting to blow the leaves off their tree
exposing bejeweled bulbs on craggy limbs
an oddly beautiful barren display

such a reliable tree noting
how swiftly seasons pass
summer yields
to fall's festival of growth
fall to its bounty of cold sweet fruit
quiescent winter to embryo buds

and I,
having lived another year
even faster than the one before,
stop to notice
persimmons are coming again

Aunt Madge

She didn't look like the rest of us
she didn't have our Italian blood
in contrast to our olive skin
dark hair brown eyes
her eyes were blue her cheeks
were rosy on white ruddy skin
her curly hair the color of summer.
She married my uncle Bill
my mother's younger brother.

Aunt Marge never joined the church
she lived unburdened by transgression.
Righteously judged by the family as a
silly senseless sinner
unworthy of redemption.
I was only ten years old
but I believed she would burn in hell
and I fervently worried about her soul.

I think she worried about mine too
chastising my pensive mirthless moods
reminding me that ten-year olds
weren't supposed to be 'nervous'
as I once professed to her I felt
dismissing my assertion as absurd
and as if she were a child herself
inviting me to play.

I recall the alien lightness
the nurturing pleasure of her company
even if some distant discomfort

pervaded our times together.
With her I had one foot in the
contradiction of unshackled exploration
the other in the special status
conferred for sanctimonious sacrifice.
I felt for the first time
the fear of condemnation
at the brink of liberation.

Too few days with her then
to notice any differences
I wonder if she knew my life was
being framed in arrant opposition
to undiscovered preferences.
Decades later I recall
the reflection she provided
I don't yet fully comprehend
but I am more childlike now
than I was when I was ten.

Jo Ann Smith

ba'shert*

there you are
exquisitely still on the water
a ghostly apparition
barely causing a ripple on the surface
my breath quickens
I lament your isolation

a white pelican
among multi-colored minions
were you exiled
not a bird of their feathers
did your coat of no color
cast you out alone
no kindred companion
no lover of your own

I remember how alone I was
before I saw my reflection
in another's eyes

wait, they're coming!
a flock of brown feathered pelicans
surround you on the feeding ground
in their midst another white pelican
she alights beside you
your great wings lift to receive her

after the clamor of splashing and gorging
your consort at your side soaring
I watch the flock follow you
deeper into the inlet until
I can no longer distinguish
you from them

from the fortune of this witness
the virtue of this moment
comes an inhale of awareness:
it was meant to be
a mystery of destiny

someone rare finds
another's life to share
scarcity yields to ba'shert

Yiddish for "that which is meant to be"

In the Light of Day, In the Dark of Night

Judy Anderson

Blood, Sweat, and Tears 1967

She leans into him, gear shift between her legs,
his hand on her thigh, the radio blaring.
He stubs out a cigarette, sings
you make me so goddamn happy…

The road ribbons through fields
so verdant her eyes tear green.
There is only the moment,
his voice, the warmth of his hand,
her tears. Torn between his profile
and the landscape, she twists,
watches the road vanish
behind them.

Like the last scene of a movie —
their heads framed in the window,
her arm around his neck, the faint hum
of the motor, the rattle and creak
of the chassis, the truck disappearing
over a rise, background score fading.

> *"I want to thank you girl,*
> *every day of my life, I want…"*

A Poem Like This

the way the wisteria drapes the trellis,
scenting the day

the way Rocket Dog smiles, then
lunges high and long for the ball

the way my grandson — the one who struggles —
hot, sweaty, and proud, holds a game ball high, hero for a day

the way words become a lullaby, a blue highway, a lazy river
benign rocking me to sleep

looking through old photos, realizing I was once beautiful
and twice loved

glimpses of my father in those photos, noticing
the absence of resentment

driving north, BB King, Bonnie Raitt,
Van Morrison for company

sometimes when beauty or pain
brings me to my knees

I write

Judy Anderson

Why I Collect Feathers

my mother returned to me as a bird
an ordinary bird, all of a single color
or so it seemed in the flurry of wing beat
her plumage befitting a pain-dulled life

yet so easily she maneuvered walls
of grief and anger, the lifelong
obstacles between us, shifting
hovering close, did she whisper?

she was gone in an instant
tipping her wing as if to wave
brilliant feathers floating
all around me

Barbara Armstrong

In the Path of Totality

Wary elk leaps the creek
jack-knifes up the embankment.
Perched among pine boughs
in the dampening light
crows grow suddenly silent.

As temperatures plummet
I slump in my lawn chair
positioned precisely
in the eerie penumbra
mark time with my pulsing heart.

Light years away
cosmic energies engage
in raging pyrotechnics
tinted lenses shield my eyes
from an explosive photosphere.

Alpha crimson slash
then the fabled diamond ring.
As light escapes through
lunar notches, sun and earth
renew their venerable vows.

I am not abandoned
but encompassed by a universe
of grand celestial spheres,
a complex choreography
stunning in its synchrony.

My breathing eases
my sense of constancy affirmed.
Resume, loud crows.
Resound, exultant ululations.
What was nearly lost is ours again.

Victor, Idaho, August 21, 2017 10:15:58 a.m.

A Self Portrait

From the Camphor Chest

Finally
my turn at the easel
before me a blank
patch of paper
like a pulled shade.
In a tray of cut milk cartons
smooth handled brushes
lean in their colors.

Almost nap time
got to hurry
right hand opts for
the mustard swirl
of a mandatory sun
a bland strip of blue calls
the lilac arc of a crescent
moon to weight the left.
Three overlapping streaks
of green complete the
grassy bottom of the frame.

I pause . . .
now for the girl
I catch her in mid-air
upside down in a cartwheel
plaid skirt blown sideways
bare feet extended to the
raw edge of sky, both hands
in contact with the earth

No pale inconsequential
hair will do but the thick
black braids of a Pocahontas,
cheeks all rosy from exertion
and the ever-present
pull of gravity.

Into the pure white interspace
a duet of watery birds in flight,
each a sweep of arches like the
cursive letter *m*.
In time they will escape the page
and fly into a broader world

     My teacher said that it was good
     but next time not to mix my colors
     She hung it on the line to dry
     beside the others

     My mother stashed it in
     the family camphor chest
     to keep it safe in case

        Someday
        I might become
        Someone
        who'd want
        to call to mind
        the magic
        that was mine
        at five

Personality Type Indicator Blueberry Packing Division

A— The Architect lines bottom of clam shell with berries of congruent dimensions. Consecutive layers replicate the pattern. No variance allowed in the weight of full containers.

Structurally pleasing result, but since
performed with meticulous intention,
additional hours may be required.

C— The Challenger seeks to establish rank and superiority persuading co-workers to engage in competition. Individual output is periodically assessed. A stopwatch may be pressed into service. No medals conferred.

This type seldom opts to return for a repeat performance.

T— The Talker instigates and maintains a running dialogue. Highly distractible and social, she packs her containers with brittle bits of national news from NPR, ring tones from her cell phone, sound effects from Prairie Home Companion, flakes of gossip, confessions, and unsolicited queries regarding personal habits.

T may register as entertaining or irritating
depending on what type *you* happen to be.

I— The Intuitive takes a holistic approach, spreading the berries like rune stones across a clean white kitchen towel. She passes the current of her palms over the congregation. Defects and rejects are discerned through tactile as well as visual examination, split or slack skins, tart redbacks hitchhiking leaf roller larvae, industrious inchworms simulating stems cannot escape her notice. She often experiences post-sorting after-images.

This type espouses sustainable farming.
Out-takes are dutifully recycled for a
waiting flock of indiscriminate hens.
The remainder,
however slight,
will be marketed.

What sort of sorter are you?

Rejection in New Guinea

You tried so hard,
so damn hard.
Pulled out all the stops:

Flashed an iridescent bib and
flared your feathers
into a black cape.
Dashing!

You danced
an artful two-step,
to the right then left,
forward then back,
and circled her,
maintaining eye contact.

No need to sing.
Any bird can sing.
Your clicking tail feathers
kept the beat.

She looked you over,
took her time —
but then she flew away.

Hey, it's not your fault,
but surely frustrating.
It didn't ask too much
of her to couple for
just a second or two.

No pleasure
for either of you
in such a short embrace.
But pleasure's not the point,
I guess.
It's just the drive, man, the drive.
You had it.
She didn't.
Take heart.

We pray for rain

We pray for rain
Grey-brown smoke swallows up our hope
Slithering susurrus air populated by mocking echoes of our mad,
    bad dreams
Tainting the sky with sorrow

We pray for rain
Blue sky in disguise
Blue denied
As a pumpkin sun punctuates the damaged sky
Shrouded in a mantle of weary, muffled light
Weak illumination with little warmth
Leaking painted despair
A cold November sky

We pray for rain
Ferocious flames cannibalize homes, bodies, beasts, trees
Habitats admit defeat, surrender, obliterated
Overcome by the savage conflagration
Frenzied gusts ingest an inferno of regrets
We pray for rain
The heavens wrapped in ghostly grey
A comforting quilt torn apart,
Shredded to reveal tattered cotton batting
Witness to disaster
Tattooed by grit and wind

We pray for rain
As dust drifts
We bear witness
Our grief and fears commingled

Tender memories split open
Revealing barely healed scars
New disaster rips our brains erupting panic and pain
Horrific destruction infuses us with fear
Whipped like weightless meringue into the atmosphere
Déjà vu

We pray for rain
Destruction is carried by the wind
Our lives are littered with the dust of California dreams
Abandoned, broken, burst
Commemorated in charred swirls
Melted metal, shards of bones
Outlines of ashes

We pray for rain
Vanquished realities, burned out, incinerated
Blown beyond the borders of towns, forests, rivers
Lives lost, lives found
Our hearts, our lungs filled to bursting with ashes and ghosts
Ignited by devilish winds
Fueled of fire born imaginings
Colored by sorrows
We pray for hope
We pray for kindness
We pray for love
We pray for rain

Today

A good day
To sit by the fire
&
dream of pending rain

A Text

I wish I was there with you
… Or …
You here with me
As I watch angels
Shimmer inside those tipsy clouds.

A.D.D.

Like a wine glass
dropped on a tile floor
uncountable tiny pieces
scatter
in every direction
some
to places unknown

If I am lucky
I sweep and gather
most of the pieces
into a tidy pile
unrecognizable
as what it once was

I remember
dropping the wine glass
though
I have forgotten
the contents
remembering
only the color
not the taste

Then on to
the next thing
which sends information
exploding like a shotgun shell
filled with bird seed
in uncontrollable directions

When I return
to thinking about
what I was thinking about
planning to have
clarity
focus
move forward
in a linear fashion
I come across
a shard of glass
suddenly remembering
the wine

Until it passes
randomly and quickly
and I am on to the next thing
though I don't remember
what it is

That Time

A story lives
behind four walls
behind closed doors
between these lines

Four wall boundaries
closed doors locked
in that place
I dream

Imagine a time
with azure skies
a turquoise sea
white sands
a warm breeze fragrance
salty aroma of sea

I was there
not imagined
but real
possibilities
of joy
I remember
that time
before walls confined
doors and windows
shuttered and locked

I was there

Invisible Ink

I write in invisible ink
the words transparent on the page
no codes to break
or cryptic messages to ponder
these words are only visible to me

They do not echo in the canyons
nor whisper in the wind
shout above the din
they are only heard by me

They are invisible
no profound epiphanies
mesmerizing phrases
or thought-provoking language

They cannot be read
they cannot be told
there is nothing to see
and eventually
these words
even become invisible to me

Faithful Photographer

The photographer sends a picture
of the full moon — are those liver spots?
And where's the smiling man I saw
as a child, a shining presence knocking
at my window —
I held the shade open
stared up at him, and thought, Yes
I know now who you are, and why
the cow would want to jump you.

It's a continual stream, his constant capture
of scenes — this morning
a smear of rainbow over Humboldt Bay
floats above the tide on its own tide
of ethereal space — reflection positive
to negative, black to red,
the wood yoyo I had
that walked the dog and spun
on its white, pure, unbroken string.

Does the photographer sleep
entwined with his camera, finger at the ready
wakening like today with rainbows,
still dreaming his dreams of yesterdays?

Waterfall of Crows

from night time roosts
full of news: everything
they've been into
mostly for food and fights

parties and match-making
and soon enough nesting,
to nourish a few good eggs
into this riotous chorus.
I tell you, Crows
we too have news
no mere cawing gab and gob,
we can stir it up like you
making of life
a clashing cacophony of sound
playing a game of murder
with our own weapons of war.

The Much More

for Fran and Madge

when the world was new
they planted a flag in the much more
spread themselves into the future
below a limitless sky

they built their home
with care and optimism
ruddy with trust in sunny days
and shiny well being

they grew to other bigger homes
but they were vandalized by time
the truth of shortening days
spread its substantive shadow

as walls of memories crumbled
they had to learn to live lightly
their home now becoming
dust powder bone

there is nothing unique in this story
or life's commanding gravitational pull
they held hands tightly
for as long
as they could

Les Bernstein

The Local Obituaries

for Davey/Davo/David

released from the dense knot of stable identity
relieved of unfinished earthly busyness
and provided a longview of shifting perspectives
the newly minted souls
unanchored from their moorings
slipped to a cushioned distance
and according to the daily news
passed peacefully to parts unknown

amid the tidy obituaries
human interest stories
national and local news
weather and movie timetables
on what page
in this squeeze of life
does one find the instructions
how to rebuild
our hearts

the newspaper neglects to say
between shadow and substance
the shuttered home of you
will be a long season
the pall will pull hard
time will arch backwards
and streams of memory
engraved in our cells
will river throughout
a span too wide

Elizabeth Black

The Fall of Icarus

Starry eyed I rise
soaring toward the future
a blissful union with the sun
Higher and higher
delirious intoxicated
heedless of my burning wings
until they shear off
Painfully I fall
my future receding
Iced with regret
I hit the ground shattered
There is only
now

Elizabeth Black

What I Learned from the Naked Ladies

I remember
reading poetry to my lover
one morning in bed
naked and vulnerable
in the bright winter light
when he said
you know
at this point
it's not about the body

But my mind
self conscious
unobliging
went straight to my aromatic
overripe fruit of a body
and stewed

Now, in August
he fills a vase
with naked ladies
his favorite flower
the pink amaryllis

Their unassuming green bodies
go unnoticed
in the competition of spring
and then
in the waste of summer
their bodies die off
only to give way
to graceful and extravagant

pink blooms
rising bravely
incongruously
from the parched earth

He's right, you know
it's not about the body
the body comes and goes
but the fragrant spirit
blooms and thrives
despite apparent conditions
or perhaps
because of them

A Prayer

Don't play hide and seek with me
instead, come face to face

Split me open
pour me out
so all that's left is

grace

Love Waits

Love waits
patient, unseen, outside of time
It cloaks as car accident
chronic illness or grief
starry night, baby's breath or
first ripe raspberry in spring

It is waiting
for you
for you to turn around
to finally turn inside

Unlike partnership, at best
a luscious rampant garden
filled with hidden delight—
still
in all its fullness a mere reflection
temporary and time-bound for loss

Love waits
for you
for you to turn around
to finally turn inside

Shredded by Loss

Hot, fierce, unrelenting
wind blows toward us
blackened Bible page
charred shopping list
tatters of lives flutter
nine miles from the fire
nine miles

What of my missing friend
rural, within the firestorm
no contact
in the dark I lie awake
ten protracted nights
ten nights

Family arrives
their prime interest
driving through the ravaged burn
disbelief hangs — what is that
curiosity commiseration or
thank-god-it's-not-me?

We are shredded by loss
innocence wrenched away
dry seasons are not benign
now we know
ashes of animals, people
rain down too
we breathe each other in

Dance of Light

Circle of light
line through time
breath on canvas
yellow blue purple
spun from white.
Empty space
made whole
by imagination
invoking Spirit
to dance.
Dust whirls
around me
a dervish twirls
to a place
devoid of sorrow
and regrets for
what is not.
Colors radiate
then slowly return
as points of light.

Jan Boddie

Unexpected Intersections

As a child I was chilled from the darkness of each death,
my eyes fixed on adults dressed in black, standing
stiff, weary from silenced tears stacked in their chests

As a teenager I experienced death with every move
to a new home, always in the summer, dragged
away from friends and teachers without one goodbye

As a young adult my questions were dismissed, tossed
into a deep hole that fed frustration, grew fear as
death's new name haunted me, a killer called cancer

Now an elder alive longer than ever imagined, I listen
to spirit, speak to my soul, dig deeper, thank death
for lifting the veil, showing its shining loving healing light

When I Taught the Unprepared Student

...in homage to Walt Whitman

When I taught the unprepared student,
When his writing arranged itself in fits and starts before me,
When I was shown his random notes and spotty attendance,
When I standing, heard the student struggle
with much consternation in the classroom,
How soon accountable,
I became tired and scared,
Till a rising flame of feeling worked me into a zone,
Where light and darkness had just the right slant from time to time,
And I look'd up to find perfect learning.

Listening to a Sincere but Damn Depressing Poet Read at Length

I want to not write
like the spirit or some trapped animals
or even dawn

I want to write like a clown car
the action popping from doors
a yellow metaphor
an orange noun
a peacock insight

the crowd roars
with grins and giggles
the alliteration pushes the car
across all 3 rings
it is our circus

these are our monkeys
they wear hats
wings
swoop up though the big tent

land on the shoulders
of the clowns
chattering, adding to the noise
the dazzle of nostalgia

the tricks — the treats
kettle corn
cotton candy
peanuts

a big tumble of verbs
a balancing with no net or references
a swan dive of insight
landing inches short of hard cynicism

you may get sick
but what a show.

The Crows

They were back early this week.
They came on God's first day, before
light scattered darkness, before
earth parted water, before
shadows grew flesh.

The crows cawed loudly, circling
the dove spied on the country road:
splayed feathers, no heartbeat.

The crows will always be back,
feeding on the light left, casting
beak-hacked rags of rays, their caws
louder by reverb. Nobody
listens: still sound? So death.

The Picnic Table

We leave the doctor's office in silence, spent as empty saline bags.
We entered in early afternoon, it is evening now. Is it the same day
    or a different life?

In the car, my eyelids drop, shutters rolling down at the end of
    store hours.
My mind a tabula rasa, except for the certainty of love.

I was running in the park. Leaf litter, mud, puddles. Legacy from
    a storm just passed.
Fog condensed into stars, stuck

to my jacket, clung to my swinging body. At each inhalation
I drank the scent of newborn grass.

A picnic table, upholstered with moss.
How many rainstorms has it weathered? Forest, I prayed, heal him
    now.

We arrive. I hoist my heavy heart and open the garage door.
Wind, uncloud his sky.

Heart Beat

The drum records the heart beat
the stroke that says
yes, life still exists.
Beat, dip, beat.

But it is inbetween
those definitive beats
that we truly measure
the moments,

the silent stretches that signify
mind, memory, life.
The machine does not
acknowledge the power

of the dips, of the way
you looked when I first saw you,
when you didn't know
I was looking,

and later, when you knew,
when we watched
the falling stars
one after another, falling

but never landing
and we, safe on that green
hillside, warm in the
cooling air, hundreds

and thousands of beats
still to come
eyes on the stars,
falling in the dark beauty,

knowing in that moment
between strokes,
we, like the stars,
would never land.

Final Eclipse

I

That first eclipse
shuttered the sun
its colors purpled
the skydark air
stars trembled
and the people
stood still

II

when the sun
disappeared
during the hunt
the mastodon
found refuge
in the wide open
space

the people watched
the mountain
fall into the water
as the penumbra
darkened the plain
between the shadow
of the moon
and the hidden sun

birds searching
for their nests
swept the sky
in great scarves
of ravened geometry
and the people
covered their eyes

III

eons later
what does it matter
to know that exotic particles
operate against the wishes
of gravity
when you see
the world
you have lived in
all these years
darken
before your eyes

you scan
the sky for birds
but they have all
flown toward the moon

and you know
you are
completely
inextricably
alone

Triptych

Shadowed Stones

We find our stories
like stones
shadowed pieces
of our lives
familiar
as breath
like grandmothers
who come
for winter
and share our beds

The Woman with the Shawl

Lazurite necklace
Vermeer blue
shoulders
"mujer del ruboso"
the woman
of moment and myth
our lifetime
told by her history
softly flecked
gold dust at her
stone feet

Avebury

We walk between
giant monoliths
a circle
ever-changing

light
to
dark
at dusk
we hear
ancient music
legendary sounds
shaped by shadow
deep in the consciousness
of stone

Walking the Labyrinth

We drive to Calistoga, walk to the end of the shops,
and discover, in a great gravel lot, a circle.
Circles within circles. And then we see it, the maze.
We walk through the labyrinth of stones,
following the path around and around,
turning back and around again in the manner
of the people who lived here before the town
grew up around this relic. Once inside the path,
the sounds of the street fade. We walk in unison.
I place my feet where yours have just been.
Unbidden, unspoken, we invoke her name—the artist,
friend, teacher, the one who was always younger than we,
even as she coped with the death of her husband
the year before. She had just begun to travel her own
labyrinth, to paint the world as she saw it, her slanted
vision allowing her to see shape and color in a deeply
personal way. Silently, we speak her name, feel her spirit
with us as we walk. Wonder why.

> in Memory of Cathy Greenbaum
> Artist, Teacher, Friend

The Persistence of Crow

The shimmering mist of identity
haunted the white bird
of no name who yearned
to belong like the majestic raven
who sang to the wolves
and led them to their food.

Not being a mythical magical bird
she tried on name after name
but none suited this persistent
white bird, ravenlike yes in her
neck and beak, but shorter bodied.
with wings that dripped
water on the sand.

Am I related to anyone,
she asked, eyes on the raven.
it's tempting to believe
but more
than possibly true

She never forgets a face
knows who has been kind
and mourns when one of her band
has been killed. her caws can
lance the air with idiosyncratic noise

One day she noticed
inkblots on the sand
where water dripped
from her wings.
usually just pinpricks,

but now words began to form
obsidian in their opacity
Look, cried the raven, your
feathers are darker than mine
almost purple in the sun
and the water dripping
from your wings
has spelled out your name

CROW, it says. cousin of the raven,
the magpie, and others of our great
family. They call us corvids
and you are the most gifted of all.

True black now marks her feathers
as if she had turned herself inside out
CROW marveled at her newfound
talent, and joined with others
who do not caw but write
strange and beautiful words
poems called onward by spirits

Still, when the moon rises full
she sometimes combs in secret
the pure white shafts of her tail feathers
with bits of emerald
and sapphire
catching the first glints
of morning. before falling
into shadow

Winter Song

The willows weep; their tears anoint the river.
An owl at midnight squatting on a fence
Sees something creeping; silent in the shadows.
Dark footprints form a pattern in the snow
All else is sleeping; dreaming; it is winter.
The landscape of my heart is cold and barren.

Beyond the banks the fields lie brown and barren;
All is still beside the frozen river.
Can there be movement in the dark of winter?
My heart is mute and still; a weathered fence.
The sky is dark. The moon is chaste as snow;
A wispy fog meanders through the shadows.

My heart a blur within the sleeping shadows;
A stuttering call—all else is still and barren.
What waits for birth beneath the shroud of snow?
Can there be life inside the ice-bound river?
Auroral light is grey upon the fence
A rooster crows—proclaiming end of winter?

What message, Boreas, from winter?
Morning light intensifies the shadows.
The whistling wind a pathway through the fence
Seeds are bursting though the ground is barren.
My heart awakes as stars melt in the river
And fall upon the pristine drifts of snow.

A fox darts swiftly through the snow,
His movement cutting silhouettes of winter.
Sonatina sounds in splashing river;

Quiet strength within the dormant shadows
My heart draws breath although my sight is barren.
I seek protection in a withered fence.
A chrysalis hangs suspended on the fence

My heart is tender as the fleecy snow.
I wonder, can my grieving heart be barren?
If spring arrives, is that not the end of winter?
My heart contains both mid-day sun and shadows
I weep beside the ever-changing river.

My fenced-in heart finds grace beside the gurgling river
My once-barren, newborn heart emerges from the shadows
And sees the beauty of the snow in winter.

Feminine Fable of Creativity

Once upon a time, long before Neil Armstrong's giant step, and
    long, long after gases exploded
off the sun, smashed together, and found their orbits on the edge
    of gravity, Eve, sitting in
moonshadow of a coconut tree, gazed one night at the full, round
    mirror in the sky and sighed,
Something about symmetry.
A milk white stone reflecting its motherlight blinked from the
    beach. A crab peered from her
hole in the sand, waddled out, grazed the stone with a claw, and
    scurried sideways to the shoreline.
The stone, set in motion by the crab, slid and rolled on the damp
    sloping sand, stopping at the
water's edge. Eve watched, pondering all this in her heart.
Something about movement.
A coconut fell, bounced off the sand, and rolled to the sea. And
    just as gentle waves arise from
the deep, lap on the sand and then silently return, the seed of a
    question began to form,
was dimly heard, then swallowed into the depths of her mind.
Something about roundness.
Many many times the moon, caught in earthshadow, dwindled,
    darkened, dilated,
teaching Eve about cycles; and she loved each phase. But when the
    moon was full,
that was the time she loved best. And she danced and laughed and
    sang and did
cartwheels in the moonlight; and the question slowly grew into
    the beginning of an idea.
Something about cycles.
One night, seeing a coconut which had separated from its hairy
    hull — a smooth sphere,

brown like her skin, smelling of starlight — she kicked it as she
    walked through the grove

to the sea. And in her mind, the gestating idea was kicking, too.
Something about turning.

She sought and found another coconut and standing with a foot
    on each, tried to stay on them as

they rolled; and she fell, and laughed, and tried again and again;
    until she was very tired, and

fell asleep, and began to dream of things she had never seen. She
    named them all: spinning

wheels, bicycles, roller skates, and frisbees.

As the moon slid into the sea, Eve woke starry-eyed, and roused
    her companion, to tell him

all she had seen and heard while asleep; and as the sun climbed
    out of the coconut grove,

Adam and Eve laughed and danced and sang because they knew
    their children

and every generation to come would create more and more
    complex tools,

and all would be used to make life on the earth more Wonderful.

The Harvest Moon

the Harvest Moon shines big and bright
as my heart fills with delight
decades ago in early spring
you came to me, offered this ring
the steamy summers, oh the heat!
the nights we tangled in our sheets
now we reap the harvest of it all,
the roundest moon shines on us this fall
your love for me, forever deep and true
romance, family, satisfaction — now in full bloom
so begins this cusp of life's descent,
no matter to us for we are content
your love will keep me warm
with the approach of winter's storm
life is granted to be lived
'tis because of you it's more than I dreamed
life could ever give

My Familiar

My familiar is white, an apparition timeless
calling upon the gods to tend to my safety
while perched upon crafts, my papers and ribbons
her duties continue when she curls upon my chest

Lingering at the lintel ensuring all is well
she's stealthy when guests appear
scrutinizing their intentions
a scoundrel
a sexy, languid pose; ultra-feline
a seer of unseen

curiosities come to mind, but I know it's more than that
she's my protector, my familiar, my cat

a piercing gaze, penetrates my thought
puffball of softness
warm, exposed belly, purrs

she defiantly sneaks outside, answering the moon
glamour is her secret power, completing any room
a statue of dignity and command
then frisky and teasing
skipping, hopping, jumping, chasing, hitting, batting, shredding,
    mewing
she is forever faithful, this good witch's cat

If Only

I've wished for magic spells
as clear as crystal bells
often during the years.
Conjure a magician
with whispered
mumbo-jumbo words.
All turned well,
like doves from a hat.

Such were those long days
not long ago
as my son lay dying.
Strange syllables that hymned like the sea
In a long cascade of gentle waves —
abracadabras
Presto!
to heal his broken body.

An alchemist —
I forged a shield
of strong sweet words,
As fragrant as his kitchen.
As aromatic as fresh bread
my mother baked
so long ago.
In another place;
in another time.

I longed to lay
the invoked armor
on his chest.

Chant a blessing.
Scream the words
that howled in my heart.

Struck mute.
Words failed me.
Tears evaporated before shed.
Silence followed silence.
The magic words
"my love" and "goodbye" never uttered.

Forgotten Warrior

The kitchen cabinets tremble with fright,
dishes hurl themselves on barren floors,
a boring coffee table starts rocking,
in unisons with dervish jars and bottles
spilling their terror on a worn linoleum floor.
Three goldfish rise from their glass prison call
in a radical gesture of self-expression
free to die at last.

A war-weary forgotten veteran
Once bright-eyed and innocent
Now cataracted by endless war
Sit on a bed of shards in front
of a television watching an
automated video war game titled
War Without Redemption
drinking himself to death.

Requiem for Kent

The pontiff of perigonia
pope of the plants
has died suddenly,
unexpectedly

I think I saw him—
a silver horse with streaming mane
flying through the trees
headed to the mountains
to catch the last wildflowers
to float in the fog with the immortals

I will remember him
in the garden
with his faithful
their stamens straining to catch his oratorio

he was their advocate
this pope of plants
this pontiff of perigonia
and he knew them each
by their Latin name

Garden Isle

At dawn
A tree squawks
Alive
Chickens fly out
One at a time
A straggler attempts
To look like a flower

The Garden Isle
Is alive with feathered homeless
Some quite demented
Traumatized
From hurricanes'
Great Flocked Escapes

Rooster promenades
Through palmed pathways
Spilling hibiscus
Orchid
Gingered flora
Serenading any audience
After
First Herding attempted escapees
From the harem

Late Summer Heat of Holly Court

for Fran

Morning steams yellow   boils
the (yellow) dandelions   by curbside

parked blue Honda   (past forward)   Ford Falcon
    roars by with abandon   (the windows
    rolled down)
    never been caught
      (never coughed or
    sputtered over oil blends or
      additives)

poets have felt the winds &   wagon trails of Highway 66
    the country garlic and corn stands
      (with the homemade
        jams)

have smelled the roses & with gritty nose of
      hobos
   stalled by the breakdown lane
    (to gaze at a harvest moon)

      or to wallow
    under a cusp
  of moon, its sliver of silver
    and jewels of Neptune,
      Mars even Venus

pen in hand
steaming

      late summer heat

Songs of Leave-Takings

1. You, mine, my love
aloft again
Chicagoland
silent goodbye sweet
clasp of hand
pre-dawn
slumber.

II. Half asleep, I ponder
why do you have
to put your shoes
on while seated
on the bedside? — the
wave swells surely
enough to
capsize this
boat.

III. The gray dawn
filters in to
quietude of room —
the birds chatter so —
robins, jays, some owl
with eyes closed too,
hoots hoots.

IV. The refrigerator's empty — I take note —
the mouse visitings upon the range —
the three traps you set —
still empty.

Master of Out of Sight

I.

Where the noon light falls
in the garden,   directly
upon heads of lettuce

and overhead upon chicken coop,
the tin roof of barn,   cabbage,
the over-ripe tomatoes

clusters of concord grapes, trailing vines of
cucumbers & zucchini,   seeds of

the caught rats you imagine,   wriggling
the carefully laid traps
along the walls of the barn

—their tunneled holes below,
the ever-crafty

and the funny names you can make up
for people you've met,   like squirrel—
      or frog

and it's not just in children's books, those
whom you wish to name!
a wind-in-the-willows kind of mind

or paint into cubes & refractions of
light,   what could be a face—
or mask

and where do you store the face
of a grandmother or mother

where can you hide those stern
or those too uncomfortable
    what tunnel

II.

Into Mind

And the shame.   Buried deep within
stomachfuls of dirt, throatfuls
of gravel

"Thou shalt forgive me" Hester Prynne
cried in *The Scarlet Letter*

scars & marks under
sleeves,   beneath carpets under the
rose bouquets of wallpaper, grandmother's

moments deep down
    on the floor of the sea
your sea-bed knees bend
lungs fill with brine,   exhale in even time

the very womb that brought you
    to bear,   brought you to utter
first word   baby Neanderthal

the grain that's always missing, the
    stolen muffins, the rats there
aboard junks that once roved the China Seas

as caliphates wandered the Gobi desert and
eastern steppes upon camels   sandstorms

blinding eyes,　　　　　heads bowed

the strife　　discomfort, the distance
between childhood & adulthood
physical distance,　　light years

the petals of dahlias lucid and
cupped towards slant of moon rays
the zinnias shine

as rats scurry
for remains of
　　　　　　compost strewn

Morning Monet

A Monet morning,
yellow wildflowers tipping hats,
Redwoods ruffling,
their needles stroking the sky;
the sea,
blue silk, white lace.

A robin scans for worms.
A gopher shovels up light;
squirrels chase,
deer graze, hawks
dive for breakfast.

Do the young see this Impressionistic day?
I did not—not then.
I saw slights and blemishes,
the daunting rain,
those insurmountable tests,
the humiliation of dancing—and stepping on toes.

I knew no flower (personally) by name,
knew no grace, (even my own),
saw no art in the mirror, (even the wide green eyes)
felt no serenity in the oak-studded gold hills (that surround),
no reflection of Monet in the blackbird (chattering) pond.

But now—Ah!—awe (awe) for this Monet morning.

Dear Woman-Child Mine:

How do I answer?
How do I advise you
on life, love, men?

How do I convey in simple English
the wisdom I've gained in forty years,
if indeed it is wisdom, not paranoia or folly,
wisdom ceded somewhere inside me
in some unidentifiable, volatile spot,
like the soft spot of a new babe's skull,
yet forming, always open to injury, death?

How do I know what will help,
what in my generation will be relevant to yours,
what of the sixties madness is not prologue
to the analyzed, data-based eighties?
How can the struggle to retain virginity
bear upon the struggle to gain identity?
How can I, more than Sappho, know your truth?

How and where do I search for patience
to bequeath to you; or, must I send you searching
into your own cavernous depths with no candles,
no matches, only the promise of sharp promontories
and the bat-like sense all women possess,
which can be and is oft fouled by *fire i' the blood*?

How can I humble myself to say, "I am of no use,
except as the spirit of Iris, to send rainbows
after downpours, to say
"I offer the warmth of my hand
until is it cold and limp"?

How then will you find my words, in the metaphors
of my existence—in purple stones set in gold;
in images of silver dust on papyrus;
in tiny etchings on cerebral tissue that will
one day, too, pass away?

Now, I can only be here for you,
understanding, not your words, but your pain,
your dilemma, your youthful struggle
with these inherited passions,
even as I
understand my own fear—of my loosening skin.

Down the Closing

Down goes
the sun
ablaze
down
afire
aquarium
ocean
affix
the emerald
flash alight
then
down

Down touch
the gray fog plateau
a paradoxical perimeter
reaching toward everywhere
the ranging herds
along slope's trawl
in the dappling mist
and going along
reap the keen strands
kissed
the droplet treasure,
pleasure
on the tongue
a momentary freedom
as he'd forgotten
when trust
had drained into
its grave,

the last breath
down
at sorrow's sharp edge
before light's last ascent
before the night
cawed the last
raven's flight
or a poppy
closing in on itself

Jeffrey Goldman

Couch

I have this secret lover
Shhhh don't tell my wife
You know, this secret lover
Kinda snuck into my life

After dinner's over
Just before the dishes are done
I hear her beckon call
Asking me to come

Into another room
And lie between her arms
To rest and melt the day away
She really means me no harm

Then in the distance I hear
Something has been said
Like "You're snoring again"
"Maybe you should go to bed"

The affair has been discovered
My lover and I must part
The hardest thing I'll ever do
From my couch I must depart

Well, until tomorrow
When she calls again
Promising sweet dreams
A new love affair begins

Precious things

Precious things
Not diamonds or gold
Things in your heart
So hard to hold
A walk in the woods
Rain on your face
Watching a sunset
Your favorite place
A newborns cry
The toddlers laugh
Time out of mind
As the hours flow past
A glorious victory
The incredible defeat
All loose luster
All are fleet
The wonder of it all
These precious things we seek
As we wander through life
The ones we keep
Buried deep in your heart
Ones you can't hold
But they do keep you warm
When your world turns cold
Like the love of another
Food for the soul
These precious things
That are so hard to hold

Murder

Black eyes bead
Voices low and deep
Related
Rustling
Uneasy
A murder
High
In the redwood trees

I am a Woman

I am a woman.
I am not my history.
I am not my past.
Nor am I society's imitation of what a woman should be.
I am not a cultural stereotype, bias, clone or replica.
I am a woman.

I am not what you think I am.
I am the trees.
I am the wind.
I am the luscious green rolling hills.
I am the blue ocean.
I am the eagle soaring.
I am the Native Flute's musical rhythm.
I am a juicy piece of fruit.

I am a woman.
I am a woman.
Alive.
Open.
Radiant.
Wise.
Creative.
Opinionated.

Able to love and be loved.
Able to use my senses for my delight.
Able to see and admire the beauty within myself.
Able to embrace my worthiness.
Able to say "No" when I mean no, and say "Yes" when I mean yes.

I am not all those things society has conjured up for me to be.

I am not mesmerized or seduced by the media's hypnotic trance. I am not a weakling.

I am not intimidated by pressures, commands, demands and hostilities.

I am not afraid.

I am not afraid to stand up for myself.

I am not afraid to be me, no longer the small person living in the box,

the imaginary box of passivity and fear.

I am free.

I am empowered.

I am as stunning as a rare cut diamond.

See me!

See me!

I am a woman.

I am a woman.

I am a free woman!

Spring Song

A fierce mantid grasps a naked twig,
divining in her garden the faint specter of spring.
She broods, then flings five hundred orphan eggs
all massed at the wind cold wall.
Her brawny pincer forelegs ape piety
as she waits, leaflike, for her helpless prey
Her jaws grind slow rapacious circles.

This slender warrior waits to eat her mate.
She camouflages hate with flower hues,
the colors of loyalty and deep love.
The male stumbles, blind and cold,
into her webbed nest.
She moves to break his fall,
to break him, and black eyes watch
from out one thousand glassy panes.

They watch the praying mantis,
the eggs all dying in the wind,
her maw, her long prothorax,
her tensile life, his thorns.

Stars of Heaven

The sky opens above me.
It is so beautiful that
I hold my breath. It
arches, reaches, sparkles.
It is so deep that I cannot see
its end. It sucks me
into its black depths — it
pulls and compels me until
I am whirled there, my eyes
agape and my mouth wide open.
I am there, in the holes
between the stars, in the black
space of loneliness,
in the white-hot coldness,
in the brilliant white void,
in the dazzling, speckled black.
Velvet dew-drop stars, electric stars,
pulses of neurons, flash in black cloth.
Steel scissors flash somewhere,
and tiny snowflakes fall to earth.
My soul is flat against the heavens
and I am sucked into a universal blackness.
I am lost among pure white stars, all
so small that the sands dwarf them.
This is not the white and black of allegory,
but a pageant of unending night.

1 January 2016

I lie in bed, watching
the way the sun burns
the frost off the green tarp
covering the Meyer lemon,
yellow wispy curls
tumbling over and over
themselves, cold tendrils
drifting toward the sky,
the most winter
can do here.

Like fire but cold.
Like heaven but earth.
Ephemeral, insubstantial,
foregone ghosts looking
for home, tenuous
memories of a year
that also rose to the sky
leaving barely a trace.

Light glazes the iron
table, sheen of sun
rays, cold patina
of January, transmutation
of solids to feathered
gas, resurrection.

Heat

Everything burns eventually
memories scorched in
seconds never forgot
days which should have held
are less than ash

emotion flares
burning into your brain
intangibles
images less than a blink of spark

bridges you won't help me build
cobalt in the blazing sun

everything filters
through the devil you know
seared into your skin
scars no one can see
knotted
twisted deep

everything burns eventually
happy times turned acid sour
undergrowth of hope decimated
by careless act of shunning

salt of the sea entering incisions
self-made when air was fresh
heated metal marking visual frustration
things too much to hold

nowhere to run
lashing out in release
before insides crisp

don't try to fix me
I need to be broken

Bound

After the fire fades,
I'm left with torn pages
coals of hope
scattered like glittered stars
wandering through patches
of dandelion fluff
waiting to be wished on
with mustard seed faith
decades old
still fertile

my name reflected
I hold a mirrored box of infinity
tethered to the tree of life
rolling canyons echo with rain
Celtic wildness calling

Painting Flowers

Lately I've been painting flowers,
colorful abstractions
unlike my usual, edgy fare.
Perhaps the garden taking shape
around my home
is shaping me.
Hard lava rock replaced
by blooming plants
whose names I can't pronounce
except for lilies —
them I know.

Whorls of color spill onto paper.
Demand ink.
Demand paint.
Demand a different way of making art.
My mother would have loved this style,
but she was gone
before I painted flowers.

Pamela Heck

Abstract

Just a pattern —
squares and circles,
lines and dots,
A theme?
A meaning?
Both elude me.
Still, I think, some message needs
to find a place —
one Chinese symbol
added to the mix.
"Love" the stencil says.
I appreciate the translation,
otherwise I'd wonder
if the sign said "pickle"
and polite Chinese men
might snicker in their sleeves
to spare my feelings.

Pamela Heck

Age Taunts Me

Age taunts me with the things
I cannot have.
It dangles pretty boys
who call me "ma'am."
If they but knew,
they'd blush or laugh
to find themselves revealed,
nude studies in my mind,
wondering if I'm the rule
and not the exception,
horror struck to think
that hordes of aging women,
whom they'd deemed refined,
might undress them with impunity.
Little old ladies in the park could make them shudder
with a glance,
worried what old folks might do
if they had the chance.

Airport Café

Greasy grill smoke,
scrambled music and banter,
backdrop for a
traveler's lament.
I perch at the counter
across from dish clatter,
cooks' chatter,
phones plugged in
for a precious charge
before the next flight.
Salad and drink
might give me reason
to avoid impatience.
You see, I'm missing home:

> Familiar car nestled in messy garage,
> lumpy bed that knows my curves,
> freedom from maps and plans,
> clothes that need a wash,
> nighttime creaks and crickets,
> backdrop for a
> homebody's happiness.

Masquerade

tomorrow never comes
promises like coins in a piggy bank:
someday I'll change jobs
someday I'll ask her out
have a child, reach for happy
or just pretend
someday I'll travel abroad
open myself to the world
or say I'm fine, thanks anyway
someday I'll finish my degree
write a book, create a legacy
or play games, turn on the tv
someday I'll lose the pounds
give up smokes and booze
honor my body, or say
I just can't change my ways

we put off challenges
want it easy
skip embarrassment
avoid pain now
for a lifetime of dismay
we stay safe and get
nowhere

believing we'll be here
forever
we wait
until our precious moments
are all used up —
immortals
we
are
not

Barbara Hirschfeld

While David Picks Olives in France

This is what I wanted,
this silence.
After the movie plot fades,
there is only this deep pungent silence
stained olive black.

The husband's gone to France
to help with the harvest.
He enjoys being productive
on his vacation.
I do not. At least I think I don't,
yet here I am
wishing I could do more.
Always there's more to do.

I let him go without me this year.
"I need the space and time alone,"
and then this silence descends.
I am alone with my thoughts—I wanted this?
alone with not knowing
what my mind can conjure
alone with my paintbrush of a keyboard
calling up what's inside
pushing this dot of finality along the page searching for an endstop.

This is just my first day,
like stepping into
a different atmosphere.
It's lonely.
I already ate a bowl of granola with milk (not on my food plan)
roamed the kitchen seeking solace, seeking distraction

yet when he was here, he was the resented distraction.
I asked for this loneliness. I asked for it.

Fog settles around our home,
a soft grace
a gentle silence
a liminal moment
between possibilities.

This is what I wanted.

Barbara Hirschfeld

solicitations

the old mailbox squeaks
as you pull it open,
and collect the stack of
meaningless envelopes
all solicitations
not one personal note.

you find yourself longing
for even a gas bill
that would at least reflect
your need for warmth
balanced with
your conscientious use of energy.
make comparisons
with last year's use, remember
recent arctic winds,
in the numbers and signs
that reveal personal history,
a month of experiences.

yesterday's news
the lowest-prices-ever announcements
advertisers relying on your unceasing need
for something better than what you have,
and on your short term memory loss
to forget
that they offered the same great deal
last week;
bring it into your house and then
take it back outside to the blue bin.

the same stars, long dead,
are mocking you

on the edges of the night.
your neighbor sits in her kitchen,
her silhouette outlined by the table lamp,
slowly eating her supper
forkful by forkful.
her porch light is on so you know
she wants company,
it's your agreed upon signal.
soon she will call.
"you get it this time," your husband will say.
you pick up the phone and listen
to her stories of what she had for lunch
where she went whom she saw.
her voice like a sparrow's echo
against the canyon walls.

night encloses
neighbor and stranger
in its impenetrable dark.

the evening news offers no distraction —
endless needs of the world
bombard you like those invisible
radio waves some people can't be around anymore,
just like them you start to shake or freeze
your pin cushion heart
punctured over and over.

soon you will prepare
the ever hopeful pot of coffee,
the elixir of morning,
the promise of a new day
where everything has changed,
where nothing changes
where the stars are silent
and very far away.

Barbara Hirschfeld

Promises

scattered about my doorway like September
leaves I stumble over them
into the living room
sweep up the fragments
to keep the entrance clean.

I wish I could stack them, as I do
the magazines I vow to read on winter evenings
or that I could complete in dreams
the wishes laid beside my bed.

Edges of the pages curl
with the dampness of time
like the book left on the porch bench
caught by morning dew
now forever wrinkled
but not really read.

I sometimes leave the cupboard doors open
thinking I will come back
to finish sorting grains from nuts
to line up every type of vinegar
with special spices
planning to create
a new exotic dish for supper.

I know I will not cannot
read them, sort them, do them all
and yet I leave them,
in piles,
waiting.

The clothing hangs with hope
of clinging to a smaller body
perhaps the fashion will return
and I can dance again
as once I swung
from branches in the sun.

Every day
the light falls shorter
in my window,
I grasp for
the promise
a mirage
receding
in the pastels of sunset.

Flight Song

> "The tribes before them were acorn-eaters, harmless
> as deer. Oh, fortunate
> earth; you must find someone
> To make you bitter music; how else will you take bonds
> of the future,
> against the wolf in men's hearts?"
>
> — Robinson Jeffers, "Ascent to the Sierras"

A hundred birds
ascend as one.
Shot upward
by the scream of whistle blasts.

Their flight
is no surprise
to the muskrat
and mule deer
that took cover
at first tremble
of the tracks
that run this
steep Sierra pass.

Fathers of invention
brought machines
to kill, to ease to
spread their seed,
relentlessly
as dogs that pee
on the same tree trunks

morning after morning.
Until the air itself
transformed
into a hostile grey thing.
Until the clouds served up
the agony of swollen seas,
and the earth here dried
at times to powder.

Oh, creatures of
the earth and sky:

You've dodged
those steel jaws
and skittered from
the gun barrel's maw.
You've darted through
the unforgiving gears
of revolution.

Now heat will push you up slope,
and torrents sweep you off,
or swallow whole your prey.
Flushed from your nest,
your guideposts gone—
Don't stay:

Not here
where there is no harbor
in the highest limb.
Not wedged in a crevasse of stone—
No exit,
this is not a home.

Fly up or dance away
to the caress of exit currents
to the refuge
of the far frontiers.

This commerce gives no quarter—
it will not shatter;
not hampered by
the rust of yesterday,
nor hindered by
tomorrow's due bill,
It charges on.

Until this madness ceases—

your beady eye
your strongest launch
your fastest break

cannot escape
the smelting down
of class and order,
family, genus, species.

A Sonnet for Eurydice

Recall the time we swam beneath the wave.
We never thought of air as something we
might need, and never lived in time. The sea
was all we breathed, and all that Nature ever gave.

And then we went our separate ways. Oh, woe!
Yes, you to Hades' secret lair, and I,
while playing lyric songs, consumed, did die
a thousand deaths, each one another low.

But, when I came, at last, my life so gone,
and you fell back along our trek, you sang
out Hermes' name! Oh, he it was who turned

to look! And, as he fell, we then moved on
together to the light. Then strings did hang
above the fire...oh, where they nicely burned!

Prodigal Son

I was the prodigal son.
And when I came home,
Honestly, to give of myself,
And to care for another,
That other was my mother,
And I saw no fatted calf.

She begged me,
To bring her drugs,
To overdose,
Since I was a physician.

And I said No.
And, instead, listened
To her left big toe,
Ingrown, inflamed,
Her constant strain.

And I dug into that,
Literally, as a physician,
With nothing but my hands,
And a simple instrument.

She yelled at me,
This woman who never knew me,
This mother of mine,
With no fatted calf.

And I relieved her pain.

Why I Cry

I don't cry over losses.
I cry when reminded of love.
That it exists. That it's mine, in my heart.

I don't cry over things I've never had.
I cry for what I have right now.
In my hand. Here, in front of me.

My tears resist death and dying.
They just won't show themselves.
For injustice. Or personal wrong.

But they flow uncontrollably
At a soft loving touch.
Whispered sounds.
I'm here. No need to worry.

I don't cry at goodbyes.
But I weep for hellos.
Even if. No word was spoken.

musings on a vehicular robbery

First, the facts:
shattered, rear passenger window
- two satchels stolen
- inside were future literary works
- exact content is lost

I.

shards of stolen mumblings leave imprints that can
never moleculize
never materialize their crafted alchemy
lost in the mind maze.

vampiric thieves choked fulfillment's passage stabbed fortuity's
    womb blinded enlightenment's eyes

and I sit always ceasing
never done

II.

shards of pillaged words careen off the tongue
sliced by a man's brutality
glass crackles spew from fanged clubs rot pages raped of their verve
irreplaceable itching whose brain will never be teased enough to
    articulate
this gift of Heaven.
a comatose life as if It were invisible as if It hadn't sounded The
    Ineffable as if It hadn't ever been Here.

Natosi A.E. Johanna

my last supper as a bear

My Last Supper as a Bear
On the eve of Tuolumne snow,
I scavenge from the fleeing campers.
Eighteen winters I've trampled these woods.
Sad, sweet losses, the times have changed.

My mother fished the rumbling rivers.
She taught me which berries and roots to eat.
Too soon thereafter, these forests grew people.
Sad losses have changed the times.

I can't open cars anymore.
But some still leave out their cans.
I roll them close by and swat off the lids.
Sweet losses have changed the times.

Up ahead a tent, I smell foul humans.
What's this? Bright light and a four-legged like me.
Grumph! They're scared, they bark, I wonder why.
Sad, sweet losses, the times have changed.

Getting dark and cold these waning days,
I'll soon have to find a cave.
Will I awaken to earth's wild blessings?
Sad, sweet losses, the times haven't changed
at all.

rooted glimpses

I

a leaf falls in
my ear, dry veins, carry
the memory   Silence is
buried in the sun's scars.

II

T-I-M-B-R-R-R
the last tree is felled
one thousand years to the chip factory
decorating soilless landscapes.

III

a black hole girdles
our earth. It waits to explode
back into being. It waits
for our wiser descendants.

IV

denuded woods have shrunk
our Cenozoic spine
devoided souls have stopped
the eternal hum

V

a seed
drifts through for legs
we return to upright walk
a leaf falls in

Dragonrider

In the sky arena
we are elegance and grace,
my dragon and I.

Diving, soaring, flashing past others
on her brilliant blue wings
while my perfect aim with the gravity wand
scores us point after point.

After our team wins,
we trot proudly past the bleachers full of fans,
mostly people my size,
all cheering for us.

I am a superstar, a legend,
a role model for children
who all want to grow up to be me.

But once past the gates,
in the private cavern full of dragon-sized heated pools,
I am something more like a pet bird.

My dragon boasts loudly to her teammates
about that fake-and-roll she pulled at the last minute
while she absently reaches back to pluck me from my harness.

She sets me up on a ledge at the human level,
where we won't be underfoot among the bigger creatures.

She praises me briefly, then unbuckles the harness
and romps off into the pools
with footsteps that shake the room.

I join my own teammates,
small creatures that we are, in our own hot tubs and conversations
which we have to shout to be heard over
the sound of the *real* athletes discussing their win.

Firebirds Aren't Red

I was open-minded
when I learned that magical creatures existed.
I did half expect to see a rhino
or a one-horned goat
when my friend took me to see a unicorn,
but no
it was real.
Smaller and more delicate than I expected,
but elegant and pearlescent.

The griffin was surprisingly catlike.
The dryad was a carnivorous plant.
Even the pixies were different than I'd thought:
insect-like up close.

But the biggest surprise was the firebirds.
I expected flaming eagles,
or peacocks that glowed,
something regal.
But they were flamingos.

A glittering, honking flock of them,
wandering through a lake,
making steam rise behind them
while wisps of flame licked upward
from backs
and heads
and long curved necks.

I stared,
feeling like I should have known somehow.
Their name is literally "flaming," after all.

But as I watched one flap its wings at another,
only to slip and stumble
like a drunkard on an ice rink,
I reflected that no amount of wordplay
could have prepared me for this.

Karma Smells Like Soap

The robot is stronger than I am.
The robot is faster as well.
The robot is proud of his superiority.
The robot reminds me of it every chance he gets.

But...
The robot can't do everything I can.
The robot can't detect the smell of cleaning products.
The robot can absolutely slip on the wet floor
by the stairs
and go clattering downward
all three flights.

He'll be fine.
But...
The robot will never live this down.

Firmament

Do you have to be crazy
to see the heavens
the way Van Gogh did

an enormous yellow moon
pulsing bands of
brilliant light
clouds dipping and curling
each star electric in its beauty
Venus perpetually rising

while below it all
a cypress tree bears
silent witness
a village sleeps
still and dark

do you have to seek asylum
to capture it
blot out the rest of the world
so you can see
the divine perfection of
a starry night

Moons of Jupiter

Traveling thousands of miles
to Tanzania and back
I find myself
in the Chicago airport
after so many years

I am hit with
such strong memories
I start to weep

remembering my daughters'
small hands in mine
in the tunnel connecting
terminals B and C
the neon lights rippling out
before us
pulling us toward Texas
year after year

their eyes bright with excitement
my heart closing in protection

now, the neon tunnel delivers me
to a little café in terminal C
sitting down by the window
looking out over the barren acres
of gray tarmac

I spot the full moon
floating low on the horizon
as pale and gossamer
as the moons of Jupiter

I feel an unexpected peace
a settling of events

my years of alienation
and exile
slipping gently
below the horizon

Falling Away

what happens when
a species goes extinct
a polar bear
a seahorse
a bird

ecologists tell us
a thread comes loose
falls away
weakens the fabric
of existence

but do we feel it
know it deeply

a piece of our own being
falling away

the piece that knows
the coarse oily fur of
the underbelly
the tiny heart pulsing
through transparent body
the rush of air over
outspread wings

the pieces that were the bear
the seahorse
the bird

falling away

Sherrie Lovler

Caught in Time

It is not her story
but history.

Numbers on her arm—
a tattoo she never chose.
Always the reminder
of life taken from her.
Mother, father, brother gone.
No home to return to.
Only the promise
she made to herself
that someday
she would have
a family of her own to love.

That was her answer.
It was the only thing she knew
that could not be taken from her:
the desire to love.

And as she passed away
with her children, grandchildren,
great grandchildren by her side
she knew she had won,
and she thanked God
for the living
who carry forth the message
to never forget.

Love Waits on Welcome

Leave room for empty spaces —
the ones not filled in
with every moment.
The pause between notes
where music dwells.
The breath of air
free of its past.

Enjoy the bird's song
without knowing what bird it is.
Smell the fragrance
without naming it.
Let the mind sit
unattached, not controlling.

Let lots be vacant
appointment books unfilled.
Leave room for the unexpected
and time to welcome love.

Winter's Silence

What finally got to me
were the children
separated from their parents because, "children
can't follow their parents to jail."
To jail for what?
For not wanting to be murdered,
raped, tortured?
I respond to the appeal
to send clothes for the children
to the "justice" department.
Maybe thousands of items of clothing
will arrive from the outpouring of
human hearts.

Having the luxury of too much hot water,
my favorite sweater just shrunk
when I washed it.
Now it will fit a young one, a crying one,
to keep her warm in camp
if her crying doesn't raise her temperature enough,
if her heart is cold and empty
without her mother,
if hundreds of other crying children
can't protect her from the cold.

I want to send it anonymously
since my letter inside is unkind and I don't
trust what lists are being created.
I learn you cannot put first class stamps
on a priority mail package

and UPS wants my name and
I can't just leave a box at the post office
that's over 13 ounces.

So it's on hold.
I go back to signing petitions.
I go back to my safe life.
Yes, I will send the sweater
when I return from vacation.
When it's convenient.
And I think of the crying children and I hope
someone does something soon.
Maybe I'll post a note on Facebook
and someone else will send clothes instead.

Well of Sadness

I search for that well of sadness that others find so easily.
Where is the grief I am supposed to feel?
Where are the tears?
There is a darkness about me, I try to hide.
There is a cold emptiness living deep inside.
More than being rational.
Beyond logical.
Past indifferent.
Unfeeling.
Uncaring.
Soulless.

I'm here, join me

Corvus, circle, perch, and wait.
Sharp eyes watch for movement.
Hungry black eyes look for food.
Curious, is that water?
Call to mate, brothers, and sisters.
Children from my nest, defend me.
All are welcome.
caw, I'm here.
ca, ca, ca, I found food.
Ah, ah, ah, I found water.
caw, join me.
caaaw, I'm lonely, where is the mob?
Ahh, caw, It's dark and cold, where is the roost?
caw, I'm here.
caw, where are you?

Heartwood Aches

Coast live oak
Gangly, stout
Clenched arms
Praise the sky.
Lowered elbow invites.
Heartwood yearns.

Boy grapples up furrowed bark.
Arms outstretched,
Bare feet primate across muscled wood.
Beneath catkin-dappled light
Quick steps out.
Limb quivers.

Agile on knobby knees, he retreats.
Gnarled girth encircled
Like his bow-legged toddler self
Once sought refuge,
Your thigh embraced.
Heartwood aches.

If I could sing, California

If I could sing
If I had his marinated voice
his command
California

I would caress you
tone by sanded tone
word by weeping word

You are so beautiful
California
to me

You are so beautiful
mountain towns
artichoke fields
coastal cities
to me

Dirt roads
tree-lined streets
rumbling highways
California
to me

Can't you see
blazing landscapes
you're everything I wanted
amid the wreckage
you're everything I need

Holding hope
sifting rubble
breathing ash
you are so beautiful
California

If I could sing
If I had his growl
You are so beautiful
my home
to me

Undoing of Knots

Daylight dwells on the backs of knots —
hard hemp ends fast to a cleat —
and we, like mice, cling to their crusted coils,
clambering with our tiny hook-nail claws
to reach the other side, where night resides.

Night soothes the deep mind, like getting lost.
Night is the telescope into the figure-eight
of nothingness. It carries us out,
inverting bottom to top,
and returns us with ribbons of wand-water
streaming off our flanks.

Night is the sable pool for swimming soundless laps,
our blown-out bubbles spreading like spores
into the smooth furrows of the lake's girth.
Night is the undoing of knots,
stirring the cool depths with our feathery fingers.

The dark water is pliant as memory
and like memory, is rearranged
by our motion through it.
Stroke these lengths of night
and hear the water's voice: *I was*
and am no more. You now become
what you never were before.

Mark Meierding

Walking in January

In January's static presence,
the trees' limbs radiate
in stick bone barbs.
Above this parking lot by night,
the galaxy's contour would veil black ink
like a quicksilver ribbon;
but now, daylight hangs gray
as a calendar's vacant page.
Winter's songs are played by violas,
not instruments of the breath.

Hands in your pockets, you stare
through a school's chain link fence
at empty ball courts. No recess now.
Down an unseen street, unseen dog
barks at children who are not there.

In this moment, what do you wish for?
Flesh moving like ocean inside flesh?
A pungency of lime juice on your tongue?
Or merely a thing that is attainable?

Kinetics

Cinema can capture successions of still
photographs and by the eye's
retention of each image,
make our brains believe their geometries of motion:
clouds rift apart, and horses canter across a strand.

Similarly,
the engraver's grain-like cuts
into a wood block can reenact how
ocean's pendulous swell envelops
scarred rocks with its lavish
white claws.

In the stippled moments of *my* memory —
a scolding on the paving stones,
uprooting ropes of ivy
or Miomira in the drunken night,
one soft, lost leather wallet,
redeeming Brice's body from the pool
and a string of ants
across the black and white linoleum —
in these, may I not attempt to frame
a constellation of ends and whys,
bowstrings drawn in shadow
and arrows gone awry?

Scattered

> *Very clearly, violence is a huge driver*
> *of why these kids and other Central*
> *Americans are coming....*
> — Lisa Frydman, of Kids In Need of Defense

Groomed with wind thorns,
their baby talc is desert dust.
Some ride their nightmares
on train roofs like river rafts.

Some drag a garbage bag
with change of clothes.
Most are soda bottle-fed,
those bottles refilled with
whatever fluids: sewage,
diesel-laced water.

They come accompanied or alone.
On these shores, rude stores of manna,
cages for the refugee.

Scatter the letters,
but we will still speak their names.
Shatter the sunglasses
— can't they see at least darkly
what is plain —
the human vessel,
containing pain?

Like José, sobbing over
the stick figure "foto" of his family,
his mustachioed papa
forcibly split from him at the border,
before he was flown to a Minnesota "home."

Like Andres, always training one eye
on the person in charge,
the other looking out for
his now-vanished mother,
his brother with bullet holes,
his sister's ghost,
unquiet angels of this age.

Daughters

for Sandra Bland

*For they have sown the wind, and they
shall reap the whirlwind.* Hosea 8:7

There but for
the grace
of the color
of her skin
goes my
daughter (lively, outspoken, twenty-something, too.)

Wait…
What does grace
have to do with
skin color?

*Grace: unmerited
favor from God.*
God's picking favorites?

G-r-a-c-e:
r-a-c-e
r-a-g-e

D-a-u-g-h-t-e-r (All daughters,
I'm bargaining for you):
    h-e-a-t
h-a-t-e
May no adversaries
be packing these.

So goes a mother's prayer,
knowing how hate
can hide behind
a badge or a suit.
A sneer behind a smile.

Knowing how a daughter
will slip the knot of childhood,
broadcast her views,
drive off into her own life,
answer indignity
with indignation.

But because of her race
may be pulled over
for a broken signal,
and find herself in a cell
at the end of a makeshift rope.

P-r-a-y-e-r:
r-a-p-e
May they be spared this.

D-a-u-g-h-t-e-r:
d-e-a-t-h
May nothing hasten this.

Our history has sown a vicious wind.
Pray we remember
this promising daughter
who reaped its fatal whirl.

Dance Festival

(San Francisco, 2018)

Flamenco fills the stage,
swirling shawls, winged white fans;
Spanish guitars flirt with
billowing ruffles of red and white
skirts; feet fly in breathless crescendo.

Eskimos in fur and feathers
take center stage, wearing
visages of animals and gods,
starting in darkness, till moon
and stars shimmer on ice and snow.

Liberians wear carved wooden
helmet masks, divine spirits on
mystical visits; heralded by heartbeat
drumming, they dance at weddings
and harvest festivals, rain blessings
on a child's first day of school.

Cambodian classical dancers begin
their ritual of a thousand years,
bring gifts to an altar: lotus, jasmine;
each gesture, too, an offering,
a prayer, transforming earth to heaven,
every human soul transfigured
by the eternal, sacred spark.

Dancers of the world move from
stage to audience; clapping hands,
we all march out to the beat of drums:
congas, rawhide, log, castanets.
Beneath crystal chandeliers, we celebrate
the exotic made familiar.

We step outside, descend concrete steps
with the crowd, who one by one, pull on
coats against cold, gray fog, pull into
themselves, scatter in different directions.
We step into a taxi. An old Chinese woman,
white hair falling over hunched shoulders,
pushes a shopping cart with only a tattered
brown blanket inside. The taxi driver honks
at her, as she takes precise and measured steps.

County Fair

Sitting in the grandstand
at the Fairfield County Fair,
childhood autumn returns.
My sisters and I applaud
the marching band show,
swirling purple, maroon, and gold.
We're seventeen again.

Night falls; lights on the Ferris wheel
wink; we roam the midway, throw darts
for fluorescent-furred bears, gaze at the
funhouse, feel wet kisses of
teenaged boys we once loved.

Remembered fragrance of fried dough
and powdered sugar pulls us to
Pearce's Sugar Waffle Booth; we break
off pieces of sweet pastry, which melt
on our tongues like sacramental wafers.

This year, we've come home
to bury our mother, who for this
one moment, we can believe,
sits in her armchair by the front window,
waiting up for us, hoping we've remembered
to wear our jackets against cold October air.

It's Still Midnight

Time didn't change in the dark.
In this world, time flows forward;
despite sleight of hands on a clock's face,
midnight didn't move back an hour.

Midnight in all its mystery,
may shroud itself from sight,
call to us in different voices,
in languages of lovers, liars, fools.

Moon and even stars circle or dance.
Time, set by the master clockmaker,
marches to its own count mechanism,
immune to man's motives and machinations.

Midnight is midnight in many guises:
on Christmas Eve, a sacred mass;
a kiss atop the sparkling Eiffel Tower;
witches drawing down a full autumnal moon.

Trickster Midnight shape shifts at will,
obscures the familiar that once we knew;
clarity at noon turns to opaque gloom,
masking what's real, or false, or good.

Things that slink through the night
flourish in winter's long, dark shadows,
but Dawn, uncompromising, will bring her light
at the precise appointed hour.

Midnight, a moment on the borderland
between tomorrow and today, will never
afford us an extra hour, no matter our
maneuverings, no matter what we say.

Write me a letter

Please write me a letter —
Send me a sign —

Leave your tracks here in the sandy
margins of my heart

You don't need to spell —
sing or sign, it's not important —

Only leave a trace of yourself,
something for me to find

Unlock the puzzle,
tell me your story,
step by step,
breath by breath,
now
and always —
sign it Wild

On the Bridge

I need not struggle to survive.
Only an inner guardian
keeps me watchful, always
facing the knowledge of decline.

My parents taught me:
Life is a struggle—
build your home's foundations
on this stone: hard work
is the only truth

Waking up to see how
work and self-denial, fed by fear,
blinded me to splendor
After years alone, I learned
that plenty was all around me.

My pleasures and satisfactions
cost me nothing.
What a surprise to know
that everything I care about
is free.

The beliefs that told me
to measure every beauty out in sacrifice,
I now escape, sliding
like water under the bridge,
deep amid dark stones.

Hanging Pictures

Sedimentary art projects, left-behind layers
deposited before my daughter moved out—
figures formed in half-forgotten hours
resist telling me their secrets.

I've framed the oil pastel landscape
in pale oak; shades of trees float
over a purple-streaked field,
slender stalks their only anchor
to the plane she sketched before she filled
her page with blended color.

I tuck her drawings, pencil-gray or black-and-white
high contrast inks, into black frames
to hang in her old room, where cobalt walls
promise heavy sleep. I grip my tools
in steady hands, wire and nails
to secure each one. Afraid to lose

my unseen tether, I catch the cast-off
images adrift in her receding wake
to wrest some meaning from this fluid chaos;
how the child she was slept in this place,
how her quick awakening pushed me aside.

Blue Brush

In my childhood home We had a plastic blue hairbrush For my
mother, my sister and me Its handle was long and sleek And fit
perfectly in my mother's small hands As she worked through
the tangles That always seemed to collect In my sister's halo of
blonde curls And in my straight long brown hair Even with no
more tangles spray I whined and cried The tugs on my scalp
occupied my mind As the blue brush An extension of my mother
Had me cornered twice a day Once at night and once in the
morning I'm being as gentle as I can, she would say I don't know
if I believed her then As I do now The blue brush grew years
of grayish lint The black nylon bristles were so close together It
seemed impossible to keep it from collecting there But buying a
new brush would have seemed foolish to my parents Seeing as we
already had one that worked Only when I was in the third grade
and my sister and I got lice from school

Was the blue brush insufficient and Temporarily replaced by
a scary-looking fine-toothed Silver comb When I was ten my
mother surprised us all And left my father The blue brush went
with her To her new apartment With her new lover And there it
continued its work On the tangles in my family My sister and I
split our time Half with mom And half with dad Who had never
been on brush duty before And I imagine this is when I quickly
learned To take my mother's place as the family hairdresser In my
childhood home that was renamed "Dad's house" Soon after I
lost track of the blue brush It was gone And replaced for good By
rectangular shaped models with hard plastic bristles Eventually,
we each had our own And now They don't make them anymore
Those blue brushes That plastic style-thin, sleek, with black nylon
bristles Recently I saw one almost like it at a church bazaar full of
old things for sale

And I thought If I could see that blue brush If I could hold that blue brush And feel how it pulls at my long graying hair I might remember something About being little About what it felt like before I learned To take care of myself and my sister And I look at objects I use every day Objects that seem to be only functional And I wonder Will my children want to touch them again Someday

Faith

When I was little I asked my father Why do singers close their eyes when they sing? They hear the music better, he told me I sat on our soft brown couch And tested his theory As the stereo played I closed and opened and closed and opened My little girl brown eyes And I began to believe That the volume actually went up That the dial on our stereo was magically moving When my eyes were closed Because the music was louder The sound was somehow clearer And I knew that my dad was right I heard the music better And as I sit on my own couch now I wonder if I close my big girl brown eyes for long enough If I will be able to hear my father better Now that he's gone But things are not as clear as they were when I was little And too many times I close my eyes in anger At the unfairness of his absence Too many times I close my eyes in sadness That he is not enjoying life And that life is not enjoying him

Yet I wonder, if I can summon even a tiny bit Of the faith I had when I was little Maybe then The volume will go up

And I will hear my father say Way to go babe Like he always did when he was proud of me.

After Your Sudden Departure...

I dreamed you drove your hot-fast Fiat into Hades,
blasted past the toll booth over the new bridge,
where boat-keeper Charon shook his bony fists
at your turbos howling over the River Styx.

Then you stomped the gas when spotting Cerberus
the gate-keeper, its three dog-monster heads
snapping too late as you sped beneath its gut
to Hell's seventh ring— you damned suicides.

There you disturbed the shades' self-pity
throwing the Fiat into a power-slide,
and Dante did then admire the color of your car—
of blood and Ferraris and open scars.

i despise "bliss"...

and those
narcissistic bores,
who search for it
in their perfect career,
coffee, or gluten-free casserole

but then i ask
"what is it with me —
always the scowler?"

until i remember my love
of comforting babies
my dream to become
mythic grandfather —
to hold sick ones, the wounded,
the frightened,
enfold them with lullabies,
rock them as they fall asleep
in my arms

Sometimes

As a child I understood.
I always knocked down the castles after I built them up,
otherwise I wouldn't have enough blocks to build the next one.
Build it up, knock it down. Build it up, knock it down.
That was the rhythm of life, the excitement of discovery.

No matter how fantastic,
how incredible it looked,
at the end of the day it was time to knock it down.
Put the blocks away in their basket so they could dream together,
ready to create the next day.

As an adult I forgot those lessons.
Tried to maintain what I'd created no matter how unbalanced it got.
Keep it together,
pretend it will last forever. Pretend it will last forever,
was the new mantra.

I built the new on top of my old suffering,
the pain of perfection, the disgrace of defeat.
I started running out of blocks.
No opportunity to recycle the old patterns,
no chance to clean out the shame at the base of the castle.

Then life knocked down my castle and I remembered.
I have to let things fall apart
so they can fall into place again and again, and again.

Foolheart

Love pays no heed to sense or reason

a man as dazzling as fresh snow
a man whose smile is like the sunset
pulls me toward him with the force of magnets

I would tear the tapestry of the sky
just to look in his eyes
I would shuffle the stars
just to hold his hand

But magic evades me
I am not a goblin
And all this is
is a sad love

I perceive
A beautiful life
with him
but only in another realm

Because he doesn't even know me

And only a fool could love someone
They have never met

Tiny Jar

I hold only memories of you
in a tiny jar of non-truths
because all we have are parallel streets
fractured lives that will never meet
a love story shaped from dew

Ideas

an idea came
as a sudden thought
I asked it to stay
that I will have time for it later
when I am not so busy
when I can turn it this way and that
while holding it tenderly in my mind

when I can let it fill with words
that I will try to remember...for later
when I have time
to get to know them better

but ideas are strange and prickly
demanding my whole attention
at the exact moment they arrive
they are not satisfied to hang around
after my superficial acknowledgement
instead they quickly move across my mind
and then are gone

and I am left with a sense
of having missed something important
it is a small emptiness
still, I long to have it filled...
as an ice cream carton I take from the freezer
and open to find, only the tiniest bit of ice cream
remains

Ellie Portner

Bat Wings

I will walk on bat wings
when the wind is a silent bellows in the night sky
when insects gather as storms
and become a throbbing beast
on their dark journeys
to places I cannot know

I will be a night watchman
on my leathery perch
bat wings vibrate beneath me
I can feel the courses of hot blood
under their thin taut skin

I will spread my arms
amid a million flying insects
and feel as if I am a submarine
floating in a cartilaginous sea
a million insects will dance away
with balletic grace to let me pass

I will hear the concert of winds and wings
I will see the tiny fires in living eyes
they are stars too small to touch

Acute?

Not the morning bird's oddly pentatonic song.
That clump of tossing poppies,
flinging orange,
is about joy—not intensity.

The feather grass full of bellows
easily had by the wind,
welcomes without remorse.
So what is acute?

Truth is a dead-bang true.
Love is climactic,

So what about acute?
Each moment,
each wholly immersive moment,
pivotal and acutely leading to life.

Apple Trees and Cancer

You
holding on to life and energy
for the two of you
brandishing your own hope for the future
and for hers too,
as she finds herself captured
in a place she did not ask to go

These are the days, coming to each
of us, some sooner, but eventually to all
when memories have as much to do
with our mental health as future plans
when illness is not going to pass
when the life you've shared becomes
the fire for your optimism

Moments suspended in meaning
a time when apple trees that still blossom
take on a special glow

Love, Dog and Life

The man's mistress and dog are both growling about their feed.
Hers is a hardy yowl, the one she spits out when a man is latent,
    like when...
She moved rapidly—in the dark—with a razor.

The hound has a shrill bark. Perhaps he's steamed because the
    gang beat him
and he'd vomited up the wife's diamond ring.

The man wants to whip up some sumptuous something.
A chocolate latte or bone marrow soup
so he can chow down and then sleep,
but all he can manage is a cigarette.

He plods across the knobby carpet, along toward the back porch
where the puppy noodles are still out.
He scoops up a handful and mashes them onto the floor,
brown like chocolate, rugged like bone.

From the other room, he hears two growls.
The freakish hot day sends waves through the open window
from the cracked sidewalk below, soothing his perspiration.

As he mixes the mashed nuggets with water,
as he spreads it on top of the table,
just like the dinner long ago,
the one that caused him to live in the yard.

Morgan

A furtive glance
as though I were invisible,
he always turned away just as
my hand pointed upward to wave.

Weeks went by, a month or more
before he knew I'd seen him looking,
we, the new renters across the street,
he, the resident of over sixty years.

He nodded an acknowledgement
not nearly as welcoming
as my many waves that had gone
unrewarded.

Friday—trash day—Morgan
leaned on an emptied bin
waiting for his sprinkler cycle to end
to make a one final adjustment.

I dared to walk across the street
from my curb to his.
Enough of his pretending
he's not interested in me.

Introductions revealed names, past
occupations, former cities of residence.
Morgan's wife had "graduated" a mere three years before,
deeply rooted in his Mormon church.

At age 87, he'd had many years in retirement
from being an oral surgeon to manicuring his
immaculate front lawn and pampering
his always-blooming beds of seasonal flowers.

His four sons, raised in his pretty two-story house,
lived locally, but his cherished only daughter
lived in Utah, of course. She'd promised her mother
to take care of her dad when the time came.

Morgan invited me to his backyard to behold his fruit trees,
vegetables, and view the deep creek of Creekside Road.
He recited the history of the floods that eroded part of his yard,
the dam built in 1963, and the reason for the stairs to the creek,

the year the neighbor's pool flooded his yard,
another neighbor's cat who kept pooping in his garden
until he lit a small bag of evidence on fire on their doorstep.
I wondered if his church condoned that lesson.

We shook hands again before I returned to my side of the street.
From that day on, Morgan never missed a chance to wave,
sometimes calling hello from his front door,
always acknowledging our new friendship.

Morgan crossed the street to compliment me as
I pulled weeds from our drought-resistant yard.
"Most renters don't keep up their yards, but
I liked you from the moment we met," he said.

I cherished his beautifully-worded Christmas letter.
He sang our praises as friendly, good neighbors.
A few years later, it was time he moved to Utah.
He admitted his forgetfulness; his daughter was waiting.

Morgan rubbed Porsche's tall black ears and said good-bye.
He handed me The Book of Mormon signed
"From Morgan Ririe, 24 February 2016," I took as a
gesture of love.

His pick-up packed, towing a brimming trailer,
he drove alone straight through from here to there.
One final email announced his safe arrival after resting only
a few hours and nearly running out of gas in the middle of the night.

He attributed his safe arrival to his Heavenly Father.
Surely his stubborn determination played a significant part.
He might have been remembered as a crusty old recluse,
if I hadn't discovered he was shy and hard of hearing.

Quails' Dance

On the fence, outside my dew-streaked window,
I see bobbing black topknots
of quail menfolk,
bouncing, "Gangnam style,"
toward a chunky female.
She two-steps backward,
maybe uneasy.
Has she learned the newest moves?

Six or seven male quail strutters
flutter just above her.
Then they alight again, closer this time.
Their blue-gray breasts swell,
blending with the shadow-tinged moodiness
of the early morning.

Now their tall fluttering topknots
are electrodes,
vibrating, quivering, shivering....
Will she choose the fanciest dancer,
or the most shuddering, spasmodic topknot?
Or ... does a gray breast seduce her?
Yet, as I contemplate, I debate....
Who is seducer,
Who is seduced?

The Chinese Pistache

Impertinent, even impudent, in August,
before fall's cool nights encourage flamboyant chroma in Sonoma,

some of the pistache's leaves are shadow-tinged
in glowing reds.
But, at a quick glance,

am I witnessing
a sabotage
between berries and leaves?
The leaves (or is it the berries) are smeared in soft rose,
to strawberry smoothie,
to fiery fuchsia,
all before summer vacation's end.

It's Confucian — no, confusing!

In My Grandmother's Garden

old oak of prisms and pearls
rose bedizened tea cups
and dried flower sachets
as high as the eye can reach

blue bottles green bottles
painted medicine tins
send fine tenor tones
into shifting air

palpitations of music
in ancient roots that curl
soar and dive deep in
the earth to dream of pagodas

my great grandmother scaled
the oak when she was seven
even then the branches
were wide as a harvest table

and nine times as thick
she said it was like climbing
a grand staircase
on your knees

she was the one
who killed a rattler
by the front walk
when she was ninety

shot its head clean off
with the rifle bought
from Sears Roebuck
with her egg money

Listen

a sound
soft as breath
careful the way
it pulls the silence
around it

weaves
through the trees
like bird or sunlight
a kind of round
lowing cadence

wordless as water
with a gentle tremolo
trailing
I think it comes from
the Bishop Pines

or maybe the meadow
beyond brambled
berries
something warm
and feathered

nested in branches
hollow boned
and wakeful in the night

At Night the World is Less Plausible

folded into a matter
of darkness and shadow
color stills its ruckus

seen only in slants of light
oblong descants soon resolve
in sharps and counterpoints

the unseen shift and rustle
night remains unmoved
dark and pensive

perception stalks imagination
senses strain to probe
the precincts of sound

there is no annunciation in the dark
where shapes bent and palpable
blend in and out of separation

enter sidelong and ambiguous
along the edge and shine of certainty
slip into baffling silhouettes

the stars far away
shed so little light
full of pauses and glimmers

unlit the world becomes anonymous.

Janice Rowley

Night Times

The aged me dreads night times
Sad and lonesome-filled hours
With masked noises and darkness
Crowded and painful images
Resented and comforting.

The dogs share my night times
With cuddles in trapped covers
Hogged pillows and restlessness
Like my legs and need to stay cool.
The fan ruffles their fur.

Themes

Themes weave through my patchwork quilt
Life like woolen strands
Some, soft as yellow pansies
Glimpsed through rain-spatters
Puddled and misshapen by the wet
Only glimpsed now and then.

Some, flicks of pavonine quickness
Shoot through moodiness
Unprepared or too slow to grasp
Leaving shadows on the psyche.

Others, gaudy as a reveler at Mardi Gras
Loud and slow with the booze and music
Easy to catch and discard.
They do return, of course.

Others a mix of vivid and faded
Like an English garden between seasons
Resisting the break of spring.
Blues, lavenders and greens.
These thread through my soul
And hold me hostage.

Climb & Downfall

When does it go forward
When does it stop
When does the movement bring me close
When does it launch me far

Where is this place of beauty
I'll encounter
One day
Where is my final rest
Where is my soul finding solace
Amongst the heathens
and love spells

Of the beauty I encounter
Who will teach me to appreciate her majesty as it grows larger?

Of the pains I discover
Who will show me how to heal the bruises of the broken martyrs?

You're lost within a valley
Of desires and wonder
You're grown amongst
Leaves and weeds and redwoods
But the space is here
The time is present
The pains are whispering devilish spells
From within your inner ear

Don't listen to the spells
Don't give in to the wild temptations, you magical being,
You were made to create

And discover
You were made
To be the one who pushes limits
Who sees far and farther

You create your own spells
And the antidote to your pains
You are the one lighting the way
The one who extinguishes the heathens
That taunt you
As they play with the shadows
That come with the fading light of day

They know what they're doing
They've perfected this trade
And it's your duty to protect
Yourself
And to learn how to play the tricksters games

How you wish you knew the answers
But you've already discovered
That you possess it all
Only you can grow
And be
And learn
And live with the pains
of the heavenly climb
and the earthly downfall

Losing Control

Life is changing
and I don't know what to feel.

My heart chooses to be numb.
My mind revolves
in endless circles.

I laugh
then I become bitter,
and then I laugh again.

I wish I had better words.

This is all I can give.
This is what you will get.

Creek in Fall

Singing over the rocks

Worn smooth

Bass note here,

Soprano played there

Trickle in unison-

Mellifluous

Frost Melting

Frost melting in morning sun

Disperses droplets

Thirsty moss plays host to

Waterstrider

Waterstrider skates

across creek,

Graceful,

Oblivious

to his twin shadow

Dancing

on the creek bed below

Alicia Schooler-Hugg

Ode to Michelle

November 5, 2018

Brown baby borne
Copper-haired princess
Temper of mellow
Content just to be

Child of rare beauty
Do you dye her hair,
Curl her lashes?
Asked stunned passersby

Elementary school
Phenomenal brilliance
Satin clad spirit
Rare resilience

A teen now and stately
Woman emerging
Animal lover
They are better than people

What happened to Shelley
Cold now and still
Heart surrendered to endless time
That embraces then suffocates
Killing its own
Matricide, patricide
Suicide.

Gone now my child
Memories linger
Heart in my throat
Choking back sorrow

Grief is a monster
With an insatiable appetite
Chews up my soul
And swallows it whole

I Dream Forests of Willows

I dream forests of willows
Aspen fringed meadows sprout golden poppies
Swamps attract egrets, ghosts of white
My eyes mirror grasses

I dream sun-splashed trenches once blood drenched
Explosions, implosions entrails exposed
Does truth explode, lies implode?

Lives sync into depthless oceans
And I, a speck upon layers of time
Float into spattered eternity

The poet sleeps

The poet sleeps
between pages of eternity
Resurrects shrouded wishes
Spiraling columns of hope

On awakening
the sentinel beholds
A thousand dreams
Slithering realms of ether

Some retreat
To souls' outskirts
Lingering ethereal embryos
Await birth

Wondering

Will they emerge as
Daydream
Night dream
Nightmare?

Each nocturnal mystery
A mountain to climb
But I shall not surrender
For
I
am
the
poet.

Ave Poetica

The crow, when it talks,
sounds off with measured caws
that describe the nature of its space.
Rattles and clicks affirm its place.

The heron, when it waits
inside the slate and umber of the marsh,
takes note of everything it eyes.
It stabs the silence with a catch.

The hummingbird hovers
to tap the wellspring of a flower.
Its frenzy to extract the essence
suspends the seconds, the disbelief.

A cloud of swallows
transfixes us with imagery.
Lines pivot, swell and flock —
murmurations in an orange sky.

Screed

Once I believed I could fly   surging against treetops   with arm
strokes like the pull of oars   When we were 7 Cathy and I rubbed
our pricked fingers together and took an oath to find the exact
center of Alaska when we turned 20   At 15 I swore I would
become an *arhat* overnight in Placerita Canyon   All day I fasted
and read the *Gita* until the local ranger found me and called my
mom   Two years later I closed my eyes   stared at the sun   and
was convinced that the oily iridescence I saw was Jesus   I believed
in the efficacy of prayer   the efficiency of internal combustion
the rice-and-beans combination that would save the planet   the
long peace on earth a black president would bring

Now I believe in the politics of my backyard   The squirrels
filibuster   the crows grandstand   the turkey vultures plot takeovers
My own animal tissues count on 98.6 and 120 over 80   I
believe in the slap-dash stuck-together last-minute wham-bam
birth and sudden suicide of the world   My peek-a-boo god is
nicknamed Creatrix Cockatrice and Trickster   but she's always
PMSing   I believe in the flip-flop flim-flam   Other side of the
fly-by-night   I never know when it will hit or help   You can call
it grace or fate or random   but you'll never see It coming

Robert Shafer

A Bird at My Window

One painfully lonely day, I lay on my bed
I agonized over my hopeless situation
Suddenly, a black-mask redbird landed on my windowsill
He paused to look at me through the glass
I stayed as motionless as a corpse in a casket
That curious bird tilted his bright-red head
and stared at me with increasing interest

Breathless, I watched him
Redbird whistled like he meant to say words of comfort
I marveled at his friendly courage
If only I could have reached out and touched him
I would have shown him how gentle a human could be

I wished he'd stay at my window forever
Too soon, after one last whistle, my redbird friend turned
away from me
He launched back into flight
He disappeared from my sight

I knew Redbird didn't intend to tease and torture me
His presence made me feel part of his world
His absence left me once more abandoned

Redbird's freedom reminded me of possibility
In my happy dreams I overcame my cruel fate
I escaped from my prison
I soared up into the deep-blue sky
I flew alongside my Northern Cardinal friend.

Nature

Desperately seeking solitude and solace,
I fled into a remote wilderness
blindly I pushed myself onward,
into the unknown

I needed to get as far away as possible,
from humanity and world's endless strife
I climbed upward toward a distant
mountain summit

Exhausted,
I stopped in the middle of a beautiful
grove of towering trees
I stood silent

I listened

All around me,
birds sang and birds called
busy bees buzzed
I heard the gentle gurgle of a nearby stream,
a sound that seemed to be expressing happiness
the friendly croak of a frog
a soft breeze sighed
through the treetops

My breathing and the rustle of my clothing
became a part of this restrained symphony
I felt as if I had completely blended
into one of Earth's magical places
Like one of the nearby boulders
undisturbed for many years,
I'd become a part of nature

Nordic Impressions 2018

Bergen funicular
Seven minutes up
harbor grows tiny below
North Sea far beyond

Family biking in Copenhagen
Dad presses pedals as
mom and two kids in front box
toss waves at friends

HC Andersen's house
A short tour
busted the myth of
happy children's tales

Copenhagen surprise
Torrential downpour
greets our arrival
schlepping luggage, drenched

Stockholm streetcar encounter
We stumbled inside
unsure where to get off
I'll show you, she said

Bouquet

You wear your charisma
like a rosebud on the edge of bloom.
You're a stormy bouquet
of reds and pinks and oranges—
hiding your core of blackened thorns
and dead leaves.
You lure pollen-drunk butterflies
with your masks and disguises.
You're a rose then a daisy. A lilac. A mum.
But underneath all your ruffles, the truth lays in wait,
a Venus flytrap in petals . . .
My first mistake.

I've been clean from your sugary sweet
Ten months, three days, and four hours.
Above you I twirl, craving one taste
though my wings bear scars
and my mind's screaming, "Reckless!"
Temptation is merciless,
stalks me like a shadow.
Down I flutter . . .

I'm a butterfly drunk on your shape-shifting flowers.
You're a poppy whose dark side bleeds hypnotic concoctions—
seduce even wasps who wear crowns.
A lesson well learned, I wish I could say,
when you come to my door
with your gorgeous bouquet.

Legacy*

> *modeled on Adam Zagajewski's, "Try to Praise the*
> *Mutilated World"*
>
> *translated by: Clare Cavanagh*

Try to praise the mutilated world.
Remember ancient redwoods
and misted ridges, sun's rays piercing the gray.
Moss patched places of silent wonder
covering long-forgotten graves.
You must praise the mutilated world.
You watched each other flourish,
dance and create your lives
one remains, the other gone.
You've seen the suffering overtake
You've heard the sound of pain
its relief short yet serene.
You should praise the mutilated world.
Remember the heart's moments that
stopped and started the tears.
Return in thought to the click of castanets.
You danced your story on the bright-lit stage
while the guitar strummed passion for the living.
Praise the mutilated world
and the shed snakeskin,
and the rebirth that enlivens, dies
and returns.

*Zagajewski's words are italicized.

The Good Book

Sacrifice your darlings
let the demons be
redeem the redeemable.

Storyline resurrection
through chapter and verse
creation's plot whole.

The Word is with the editor
and the editor is the word
reorganized on the page.

Crucify the phrase
a writer's cross to bear
the gospel of revision.

Novel expressions
a parable complete
the book, a revelation.

Deborah Taylor-French

What the Romans Knew

All along the road,
the two-faced god—Janus,
sees forward, and backward.
Stone pathways build resolve
each step a beginning and an end.

Yet I look back at what has passed.
Puzzled, not knowing the price of a glance.
The past fails to tell my fortune.
Rival points of view stymie as
the future addles my present.

A persistence of vision narrows choice of passage.

Being mortal, I read Homer,
Hesiod and Sappho,
enthralled by
their vitality,
and verisimilitude.

On the Roman road, long buried,
the craft of departed engineers
and stone masons defies fate.
They crafted these *iters* for
the reach of their wagons.

Unknowingly, they invented the track
span for modern trains. This cart roadway,
cut and laid stone by stone in the 3rd century
lies perfectly level. Firm under foot
as if I were the first to tread this way.

The Enormity of Night on a Roman Bridge

Sunset, people stroll dreamlike near
the solemn Mosque-Cathedral of Córdoba.
A lithe violinist plays a sonata, which
resounds inside the war memorial arch.

Within medieval walls, twilight gilds
the dusty haze illumined by streetlamps.
Night awakens a cloud of bats.
Rising black angels lift my gaze to heaven.

We amble onto the Roman bridge,
its watchtower cloaked in indigo skies.
The Roman sentry tower stands locked.
Dark windows absorb light like a Dutch painter's eyes.

Guadalquivir, Great River in Arabic,
cuts a sinewy course in southern Spain,
its gifts sculpt a four-hundred-mile Garden of Eden,
which then flows into the Atlantic.

In the darksome waters, timbers lean from a swamped
Roman waterwheel, a haunted draw for obsessed oil painters.
The broad black river recalls Vincent's question.
"When will I paint my starry night?"

Diligent to possess Chiaroscuro skills of French artists
like Millet, Corot and Courbet, Vincent van Gogh worked feverishly.
Soon he devised "The Potato Eaters." Not long afterward
in indigo oils, he embedded a night ablaze with stars.

Barbara Toboni

Morning Light

After a day of rain
I open the door
to sunlight

Crepe myrtle's
red leaves
litter the porch

Black towhee
wings to lilac
chirps brightly

The clearness
of morning light
is calling

For Father

Once at the beach
we spread straw mats
You rested
while I shoveled sand
filling and spilling my pail
until your eyes closed

A breeze chilled me
and I lay down too
Covered us both
with my mat
but the wind flapped it
like a sail

I grabbed one end
and you the other
Together we swayed in
white-capped waves
until the chuckles
of gulls woke us

Tired, Poor... and Unwanted

" Al fin en los Estados,"
so el coyote said,
"Camina detrás de esa cuesta
y verás casas y gente."

That was early in the morning
the hill is now behind,
the night is getting close,
and ahead just a vast plain.

"Mamá, ¿dónde estamos?"
asks 4-year-old Rosita.
Diego, her 10-year-old brother, replies,
"Mamá no sabe, Rosita. El coyote la engañó"

Mamá Ana's silent tears
begin to flow,
as they always did:
true and deep.

Now, she holds just one wish:
to be the last one to go,
so she could hug them
for the rest of their brief lives.

For Penelope

Because of you,
I think I'm going to travel the world.
That's right. I'm going to pack up everything
And sell it all, or give it away,
Take a giant leap and land
Where I land.
But first
I think I'll stop in Washington
And tell that guy
What I really think of him;
Of course I'll leave my kitty cats at home.
And then spring into the air
And see Europe and Africa and
Australia and Russia and Asia and
Wake up on the white sands of
The Seychelles
Drunk and drowsy on the beauty of it all.
And you'll be with me
By that shore,
And in the trees;
In the very air that I breathe.
That's what I want to do
When I think of you.

The Secret Dragon

In the summer hazy memories of my youth
We were knights, you and I. Both
With mighty wooden swords riding on
Broom-handle steeds with fiery bottle-cap-eyes.
We'd gallop and explore
The undiscovered trails,
To the vacant lots next door.

There we slayed the bad and
Saved the good.
We were the stuff of legends,
You and I.

On our street
We climbed the highest hill,
And rode our giant cardboard ships,
Like two captains on a stormy sea,
Screaming down the precipice,
Till we fell
And rolled
In an entangled clump of laughter and glee.
And never satisfied we climbed to the top
Only to scuttle down
Again and again.

On our street were
Winter castles of newly fallen snow;
Shining sparkling fortresses,
Built by the two of us,
The hero knights,
Armed with snowballs,

Standing back to back,
Surrounded by enemies,
Too scared to attack.

On our street
We were the heroes,
You and I. Yet

On our street lived
A secret dragon.

She would visit us
In the night.
Her sharp and crooked claws
Reaching down,
Pressing, smothering
The fear, the screams
That nobody heard,
Or chose not to hear.
Ripping away
Trust and tears
Leaving only a
Piece of flesh,
Betrayal and
Nightmares;
She was the dragon.

When we saw her we
Would
RUN!

. . . if we could.

When we did escape
To some secret place,
Like heroes need to do,

We ran, stumbling, through the conquered fence
To the imaginal lands a yard away.

There in our secret hide-a-way tree,
Where we flew and hung like monkeys,
Devouring the ripe, juicy, grapes
That hung in easy reach.
Our greedy little fingers;
Our mumbling mouths,
Filled till they spilled,
Running purple down our chins.
There in that
Safe and sacred spot
We'd howl at the skies
But, never, talk
Of the dragon we couldn't slay.

In our safe spot
We were the heroes,
My brother,
You and I.

Time passed.
The hero-child faded,
Left behind with forgotten toys
And stolen innocence.
Gone were the knights.
Grown were the diffident courtiers, and
Three thousand miles apart,
You reached out and
I wasn't there.

You cried pitiful tears
For the cardboard ships and
I wasn't there.
The wooden steed stood

Standing alone in the corner of your kitchen,
Lamenting the loss of the hero child and
I wasn't there.

But the dragon was . . .

Your final scream at heaven
Was a howl for peace.

So it is you are gone
And I am here.

Jim Wilder

Somewhere Near Kalihi

Young man of da land
take one girl by da han'.
He promise to be a man,
somewhere near Kalihi.

Da maiden han' he won.
Life together just begun.
Soon dey have one son,
somewhere near Kalihi.

Lots of land dey got to clear
work together, got no fear,
many laughter, little tear,
somewhere near Kalihi.

Island family grows and grows,
many fingers, many toes,
many butts and many nose,
somewhere near Kalihi.

Island house full of love,
like the rainbow up above,
or the cooing of the dove,
somewhere near Kalihi.

One day children start to go.
They own way dey must know.
They own strength dey mus' show,
somewhere near Kalihi.

One day he do not rise.
Something wrong deep inside.
Together dey all cry,
somewhere near Kalihi.

Old woman gray and bent,
her life almos' spent,
wonder where da years dun went.
somewhere near Kalihi.

Island house all broken down.
Plants again cover da groun',
Wheel of life go roun' an' roun',
somewhere near Kalihi.

Friends After Lovers

Two lonely souls crossed paths in the night
in the dark of the local saloon.
She had children almost his age.
But in the warm summer night
they didn't care what was right,
both needing to feel someone breathe.

She found a friend in the bottle,
but he came and he went
never to be trusted nor loved.
In day light she lied.
In the darkness she cried
grabbing love as it wandered by.

He came home from a war,
a soul tired and sore
with nothing to lose nor gain.
He needed something
or he needed someone
to help him escape from the pain.

With her kids off to school
and his bag of tools
they hoped the neighbors didn't know.
It was none of their business
but they wanted no witness
so they put on a respectable show.

Before their demons got too bad,
they were only too glad
to fall into each other's arms.

They became friends after lovers
beneath the soft covers
sharing fears, secrets and dreams.

With autumn's red leaves
he took to the seas.
They had done all they could for each other.
The years rolled on by
but there remained in each heart
a special place for one another.

Every year without fail
through smooth seas or gale
he'd call on the day of her birth.
Until a strange voice cried,
"I'm sorry to say but she passed away
alone in her bed just last night."

So in the spring of each year
when there is no one to hear
I whisper her name to the night.

Marion

A Late Night Jitterbug

A rose in full bloom is so beautiful
ruby lips and cheeks silky smooth
the fragrance intoxicating
no place or time for a wallflower

like the flora in a Disney Cartoon
this special flower moved to music
held the wounded in embrace
a last dance for the dying

She came to me, long wilted
her pollen played into seeds spread
across the countryside
new flowers to behold

She shared with me
the splendid flavor
of her rose hip tea
brewed carefully, a tasty blend

the tea sustained so many
the pot never went dry
we moved in jazzy rhythm
one last late evening dance

Snip

It's easy to cut his hair:
he doesn't have much.
Out on the deck
the sun waits its turn,
the air fresh and sharp.
He needs the wisps done
down by his neck
almost down his back, ugh.

I only have the pointy snips;
I'm careful, but I can be careless.
He'll really get pissed if I poke
though he's pretty tolerant
about cabinet doors left open,
outside garden faucet leaking,
post-its on his shoe as
he walks thru the house.

But no one likes to get hurt
by their love.
Though is *love*
the word to use
when you end up with
someone for 25 years and
the Sunday morning priority is
to cut each other's hair?

With each gray tuft
falling on the white sheet
I wonder
what is our trajectory?

At first, me on the keys,
he with his clarinet—
Mozart's elegance.
And now the scissors trim and clip.

I feel the light tendrils
of his hair.
Sun breaks through,
spotlights the bald dome of his head.

Poet Biographies

Judy Anderson splits her time between Marin and the Trinity wilderness where she bakes, builds rock sculptures, and dances with her muse at the edge of the river. Her poems have graced a wall in the Arbor Café in Oakland and appeared in over a dozen anthologies.

Barbara Armstrong has a lifelong interest in the nuanced power of words. Recent poems appeared in *Phoenix,* Redwood Writers 2018 anthology, and *Reverberations*, a project which resulted in a book of ekphrastic poetry and the art that inspired it. Hobbies include: gourd art, Shaker box making, music, and organic blueberry farming.

Stephen Bakalyar had a diverse writing career as a chemist, producing marketing materials and publishing research papers in scientific journals. He writes poetry, memoirs, essays and short stories. Subjects range widely from the nature of water to the history of astronomy. Stories often concern the quandaries of older men.

Judy M. Baker broke her high school gender barrier enrolling in industrial arts and printing a chapbook of her poetry and illustrations. Baker grew up reading books like most people eat popcorn, inheriting literary consumption from her parents. Communication illustrates her path: actor, graphic designer, coach, marketing strategist, teacher, author.

Margaret Barkley is a poet, teacher, and curious observer of humans and nature. She has led a writing group in her home since 1999. She has an MA in Psychology with a focus on group facilitation and has taught at SSU in the Psychology Department and Organization Development Master's Program.

Warren Bellows is an artist, poet and a retired acupuncturist who lives in West Sonoma County. He is consistently inspired by the paradisaical natural world wherein he lives.

Jory Bellsey has been writing poetry and prose since a teenager. He believes the English language has become acronyms, emoticons and fractured sentences which have diminished our ability to think and relate to one another. Poetry reminds him of the beauty of words and the need for them to be showcased.

Henri Bensussen has published poems in *Blue Mesa Review, Common Ground Review,* & *Sinister Wisdom,* among others, and in various anthologies. Finishing Line Press published her chapbook *Earning Colors* in 2015. She served on the board of the Mendocino Coast Writers Conference before moving to Santa Rosa in 2016.

Les Bernstein's poems have appeared in journals, presses and anthologies in the U.S.A. and internationally. Her chapbooks *Borderland, Naked Little Creatures* and *Amid the Din* have been published by Finishing Line Press. Les is a winner of the 6th annual Nazim Hikmet Festival. She also was a Pushcart Prize Nominee in 2015. She was the editor of the Marin Poetry Center High School Poetry Anthology and has co-edited two anthologies for Redwood Writers.

Elizabeth Black is the progeny of a family of artists and writers from California and Quebec. She is most at home communing with nature, where poetry began to arise within her when words otherwise seemed to fail. She does not claim responsibility for poetic expressions, only for pruning them to look like poems.

Skye Blaine writes fiction, memoir, and poetry. She received an MFA in Creative Writing from Antioch University. *Bound to Love: a memoir of grit and gratitude* was published in 2015. Her debut novel *Unleashed* came out in November 2017. She teaches fiction and memoir in SRJC's older adults program.

Laura Blatt has worked as a website writer, a laboratory technician, and a publishing company manager. Her writing has appeared in various venues, including *Lilith Magazine, California Quarterly, Vintage Voices,* and *Phoenix,* a poetry anthology. A member of the California Bar, she also has a master's degree in biology.

Jan Boddie, PhD, former psychotherapist and member of the first AIDS Unit Counseling Team, San Francisco General Hospital, has memoir stories published in seven anthologies and two poems published in the Redwood Writers 2018 poetry anthology *Redemption*.

Abby Lynn Bogomolny is the author of the poetry collection *People Who Do Not Exist* and the editor of the anthology *New to North America: Writing by U.S. Immigrants, Their Children and Grandchildren*. She teaches Composition, Literature and Creative Writing at Santa Rosa Junior College and lives in Northern California.

Catharine Bramkamp holds an MA in Creative Writing and a BA in English. She has written 17 novels and 3 books on writing. Her poetry has been included in a dozen anthologies including *And The Beats Go On* and the chapbook *Ammonia Sunrise* (Finishing Line Press). Her current book, *Don't Write Like We Talk,* is based on 200 plus episodes of the Newbie Writers Podcast.

Simona Carini was born in Perugia, Italy. She is a graduate of the Catholic University of the Sacred Heart (Milan, Italy) and of Mills College (Oakland, California), Simona writes nonfiction and poetry and has been published in various venues, in print and online. She works as an academic researcher in Medical Information Science. Her website is *www.simonacarini.com.*

Fran Claggett-Holland, an English and Humanities teacher and consultant for many years, now teaches poetry and memoir. She recently launched her latest book, *Moments with Madge: Lux Aterna,* a poetic and artistic tribute in honor and memory of her life partner Madge Holland. In addition to a number of books for the teaching profession, she has published two poetry books (Taurean Horn Press and Risk Press). She has co-edited two poetry anthologies for Redwood Writers.

Annita Clark-Weaver has published one memoir/biography. She writes poems, stories and letters to herself and others. She is frequently amazed by the beauty and power of words. Her favorite book is Roget's Thesaurus. She lives in Sebastopol near her son, daughter-in-law and three grandchildren who teach her about life.

Tina Riddle Deason's first novel, *One's Own Sweet Way,* a novel about anxiety disorder (written as CM Riddle), was released in 2018. She enjoys writing about everyday magic including writing and performing ritual and ceremony. She is currently working on her next book, Vineyard Road. *Priestesstina.com.*

Roger DeBeers, Sr., BA, History SFSU, MA English and MFA Creative Writing Goddard College. His varied background as an English instructor, commercial pilot, flight instructor, government functionary, househusband, single parent, layabout, remodeling contractor, Red Diaper Baby, Street Kid, Marine Corps corporal and Army Officer lends richness to his writing.

Patrice Deems, a native Californian, just began taking dozens of spiral notebooks out of the closet in 2017, when she joined the Redwood Writers. Years of poetry, song lyrics, stories, family limericks and obituaries crowd the pages. There is even an "original" musical—ten years in-the-making amongst them. No going back now.

Nancy Cavers Dougherty, a writer and artist, advocates on issues relating to child and family welfare. Nancy is the author of three chapbooks: *Tape Recorder On, Memory in Salt, Levee Town and Silk,* a collaborative work. She and her husband live on a small farm in Sebastopol.

Ida Rae Egli has two books to her credit: *No Rooms of Their Own: Women Writers of Early California* and *Gold Rush Women: Frances Fuller Victor and the New Penelope.* She has read and lectured for the Sierra Club, UC Davis, Sonoma State University, and the Orange County Festival of Women Authors. She was chair of the Santa Rosa Junior College English Department. She has had poetry and fiction published in numerous periodicals.

Christina Gleason lives in Sonoma County and writes fiction, non-fiction, essay and poetry. Her poetry has won first place in NorCal Poetry Slams. Her prose and poetry, as well as music and art, have been published. Her background includes documentary film, research and photography; sculpture and music.

Jeffrey Goldman has lived in Sonoma County for the past 28 years. He still works in Napa as a machine operator and dreams of being retired. On the weekends, during the Gray whale migration, he can be found on the Head pointing out whales to visitors from other lands, states, and countries. He writes poetry for fun.

Dianna L. Grayer, Ph.D., is a Marriage and Family Therapist. She began writing creatively in the early 90's and has published 6 children's books, a poetry book and journaling book, both with accompanying CDs, and several plays, her most well known, *Private Lives, Private Lies.* Dianna loves writing to empower and inspire.

Susan E. Gunter has published poems in journals around the country, including *Atlanta Review, Louisville Review, Poet Lore,* and *Literary Nest.* She is on the board at the Marin Poetry Center.

Karen Hayes grew up in Healdsburg, California, where she spent several formative years on the Russian River. She lives in Sonoma County, and loves spending time in Fort Bragg, California, where she gets most of her writing done. She currently has one book of poetry published, *River Stone.*

Pamela Heck is an award-winning artist, a special education teacher, and a writer of short stories, memoir, poetry and children's books. Her writing has appeared in Club anthologies, as well as in the *Literary Review.* She is currently on the Redwood Writers Board of Directors.

Lenore Hirsch, after a career in education as a teacher and administrator, writes humor features about aging for the *Napa Valley Register,* as well as poetry, short stories, food and travel pieces. In 2018, she published a poetry collection, *Leavings.* See *www.lenorehirsch.com.*

Barbara Hirschfeld has been a writer all her life and has just become interested in "coming out" in public as a poet. Her work has appeared in the Redwood Writers and the Sitting Room anthologies. She lives on eight acres in West Sebastopol and teaches meditation. She finds the process of writing poetry another valuable way to work with her mind.

Louise Hofmeister, after a long career that included lots of grant writing, decided to pursue some more creative expression upon retirement. She enjoys exploring various forms and hanging out with her poet-mentors. She had three poems in last year's anthology and three picked up for publication by *Truth Serum* and *Pure Slush.*

Jon Jackson is a retired psychiatrist who has had a lifetime interest in literature, film, and music of most kinds. He currently lives in Sebastopol, where he leads groups on film and depth psychology, and where he teaches a course on Rilke. He also does an occasional music show on KOWS FM.

Natosi A.E. Johanna has been a writer her entire life. Poetry was her first genre, but she has also penned fiction and creative nonfiction works. Natosi grew up in the pine forests of northern Minnesota, but has lived in California for the past forty years. Sonoma County has claimed her heart for the last twenty years.

Mara Lynn Johnstone grew up in a house on a hill whose top floor was built first. She lives in California with her husband, son, and laptop-loving cats. She enjoys writing, drawing, and spending hours discussing made-up things.

Briahn Kelly-Brennan's sole purpose in writing is to make her feel, when she reads it, happy, content, satisfied, astounded, dreamy, or any kind of new and wonderful emotion. Because life can be hard, what you pay attention to grows, and why not focus on the half of glass that's full?

Betty Les has been writing poetry for most of her life although she didn't always know it. Her most recent work explores the intersection of science and the mysteries of nature. She was chosen as a Redwood Writers Award of Merit Poet in 2018. Betty holds a Master's Degree in Zoology.

Sherrie Lovler's poetry is inspired by spiritual writings. Her practice is to read from various authors until something sparks in her. Then she allows a poem to flow. Sherrie is also an accomplished painter. She combines the two in her award-winning book, *On Softer Ground: Paintings, Poems and Calligraphy.*

Roger C. Lubeck is the president of the Redwood Branch of the California Writers Club. He is the publisher of It Is What it is Press. Roger's published works include seven novels, two business books, stories, poems, articles, reviews, a produced 10-minute play, and a prize-winning flash fiction.

Beth Ann Mathews, a marine biologist and educator, studied marine mammals in Alaska. From 2010 to 2013, her family sailed from Alaska to Mexico. Her upcoming memoir, *Catching the Hundred-pound Halibut,* begins when her adventurous husband suffers a brainstem stroke. She has published in *Sail Magazine, The Bubble,* and *Marine Mammal Science.*

Laura McHale Holland as a child, loved the musicality of language and often recalled, verbatim, conversations she heard. She lost that ability long ago, but her love of language remains, influencing everything she writes. All four of Laura's published books have won awards. To connect, leave a comment at *http://lauramchaleholland.com.*

Mark Meierding's poems often aim to evoke a memory, mood, or tone. Beyond that may follow an attempt to discern a pattern underlying the sensations—like seeking shapes in shifting clouds. Mark and his wife live in Rohnert Park with an odd cat, Lulu.

Phyllis Meshulam's full-length poetry book, *Land of My Father's War,* comes from Cherry Grove Collections. Her work appears in magazines from *Ars Medica* to *Teachers & Writers* and several chapbooks. She teaches with California Poets in the Schools and edited CalPoets' Poetry Crossing, "a joyful collection of lessons and poems."

Stephanie Moore is a recently retired English teacher from Santa Rosa. Her work has been published in the 2018 Redwood Writers Poetry Anthology: *Phoenix: Out of Silence...and Then,* the Marin Poetry Center Anthology, and *California Quarterly.*

Catherine Montague is a writer, professor, and researcher who divides her time between Sebastopol and Berkeley. Previous publications include poetry in the Redwood Writers *Call of the Wild* and *Phoenix: Out of Silence* anthologies and the Point Reyes Seashore Association's newsletter.

Patricia Nelson is a retired attorney and environmentalist. She has worked for many years with the Activist group of poets based in Marin County.

Remi Newman is a writer and sexuality educator living in Sonoma County. She has her master's degree in sex education from NYU and over 15 years of experience helping people live happier, healthier sex lives. She has written online articles for *Good Vibes, Kinkly, The Good Men Project* and *Together Guide.*

Michael Jack O'Brien has been submitting and publishing work for over 50 years. He still works on craft and inspiration.

Jan Ögren, MFT is an international author, developmental editor, public speaker and licensed psychotherapist. *Choose Life: Poetry, Prose and Photography* is in honor of her 100-year-old father's philosophy of life. Her novel *Dividing Worlds* was published in Brazil in 2014. *Dragon Magic: Amazing Fables for All Ages*, 2015. *www. JanOgren.net*

Renelaine Pfister's stories, essays and poems have been published in her native Philippines and in the U.S., including *Vintage Voices* 2012, 2014 and 2018, *And The Beats Go On,* YWCA's *Cry of the Nightbird, Filipino Fiction for Young Adults, Beyond Lumpia, Pansit and Seven Manangs Wild,* and *Healdsburg and Beyond.*

Ellie Portner is a morning person. Waking early she heads to her workspace to write, draw or work on her current rug-hooking project. Ellie's poetry is inspired by words, images and ideas. She writes poems about love, ideas, time and aging, dreams, her art, water and sometimes people.

Linda Loveland Reid is past president of Redwood Writers and Jack London Award recipient. She is author of two novels. With two cum laude BA degrees from SSU, she currently teaches art history for SSU and Dominican University through the Osher Lifelong Learning Institute. Linda is a figurative oil painter and theater director. (website: *LindaLovelandReid.com*)

Belinda Riehl studies and experiments with writing in her weekly poetry critique group. Her poems and short stories in fiction and memoir have been published in *Sonoma Seniors Today* and online *Medium.com* magazines, as well as Redwood Writers prose and poetry anthologies. She has enjoyed serving in numerous volunteer positions of Redwood Writers since 2014.

Jane Rinaldi is a former teacher working in several languages. It never occurred to her that she could throw her accumulated knowledge into one big washing machine to see what unexpected rhythms and rhymes would result. She is now retired, living in Santa Rosa and enjoying the inspiration of nature up close.

Margaret Rooney is a retired psychotherapist with an addiction to writing poetry. Her poetry group is helping her manage it in a positive, self-reflective way. She has published in The Redwood Writers 2018 anthology and in *Reverberations*.

Janice Rowley's curiosity has led her many places, from the rural South to the California wine country, from airline to veterinary, from show dogs to rescue dogs, from reading to writing, from memoir to poetry to fiction, from a young woman with dreams to an old lady with memories.

Jennifer Sawhney is a writer born and raised in Sonoma County who began writing poetry at age thirteen. In 2015, she challenged herself to write one poem a day, then began posting them online in 2016 and has continued ever since. She is currently working on publishing her first poetry collection.

Kathleen Scavone, MA., is a retired educator. She freelances fiction, poetry, nature writing, curriculum ideas and local history. She has self-published four books, a play and a poetry chapbook. Kathleen is a photographer and potter. Her other interests include hiking, assisting on archaeology digs, travel and volunteering for NASA.

Alicia Schooler-Hugg is a former op-ed columnist and features writer for *The (Stockton) Record, Modesto Bee, Nurseweek,* and *nurse. com.* Alicia taught university level communications courses and received several journalism-based awards. A poet and fine artist, she is published in several anthologies and has authored two books: *Art and Soul of Jazz, A Tribute to Charles Mingus, Jr.* and *Granny Does Europe: A Love Story.*

Florentia Scott worked for many years as a corporate communicator and journalist before retiring. She is writing novels and is gathering her poems into a chapbook. Her creative work has appeared in *Ascent Aspirations* magazine, the *Alberni Valley Times,* the San Francisco Writers Conference Anthology, and the Redwood Writers 2018 Poetry Anthology: *Phoenix Out of Silence.* Her work is inspired and nourished by observation and experience of nature and human relationships.

Jan Seagrave has degrees in the philosophy of religion. Her poems have appeared in the Marin Poetry Center Anthology 2016 and 2017, Redwood Writers Poetry Anthology 2018. She attended Bread Loaf Writer's conference in 1979 and won the Pony Pegasus award at the 1966 CA Chaparral Poets' Poetry Competition.

Robert Shafer, a member of Redwood Writers, grew up as a Chicago slum boy and an abandoned child. Those early years inspire much of his writing. He served four years in the US Navy and worked thirty-five-years as a film/video editor in San Francisco. He currently resides in Napa, California.

Marilyn Skinner Lanier's childhood on ranches in the 1950s' American west inspired her debut novel, *Hardpan,* published in 2015, and other short stories and non-fiction pieces. She is writing a sequel to *Hardpan* and other familial stories rooted in the west.

Jo Ann Smith spent most of her life in public education as a teacher, counselor, vice principal, principal, district administrator and for the last twelve years of her career as superintendent, all at the high school level. Now retired, she finds herself drawn to the evocative nature of poetry, a very different kind of writing specificity. This journey continues to be challenging, revealing and liberating. Jo Ann has three poems published in the Redwood Writers 2018 Poetry Anthology. She lives in Sebastopol with her partner, Gale and their two standard poodles, Gracie and Bodhi.

Robbi Sommers Bryant's award-winning books include a novella, four novels, five short-story collections, and a book of poetry. She's published in *Readers Digest, Redbook, Penthouse,* college textbooks and anthologies, and her work has been optioned for television. She served as Editor in Chief for the 2018 RW anthology and currently is Vice President of Redwood Writers. She's a developmental, content, and copy editor. *robbibryant.com*

Linda Stamps established careers in law, journalism, and higher education. Her published works include poetry and non-fiction. She is a member of Redwood Writers and the Blue Moon Salon. Her poetry is inspired by a phrase here, a word there, the unknown, and the rhythm of the heart.

Deborah Taylor-French writes mystery and poetry. Find her novel *Red Sky at Night: Dog Leader Mysteries* on Amazon. Sign up for her free newsletter, deals, and eBook samples. For more visit her blog, Dog Leader Mysteries. Learn ways to save your dog's life and your sanity, visit *www.dogleadermysteries.com.*

Barbara Toboni has published a variety of short stories and articles in anthologies and online. Her works also include three collections of poetry, *Undertow, Water Over Time*, and *Light the Way. The Bunny Poets*, a children's picture book, was published in 2018. Barbara lives in Napa Valley with her husband.

Luis Salvago-Toledo was born and raised in Málaga (Spain), where he attended the Merchant Marine Academy, Master. After sailing as a deck officer for over 10 years, he settled down in California. Here he worked in the computer field while studying philosophy (BA UCLA, MA UC Berkeley). Today a retiree, he enjoys tutoring Spanish and occasionally writing newspaper columns.

Arte L. Whyte is a writer in Sonoma County. He has published poetry, journalism and a novel, *The Children of the Stars; Book One, SAIQA*. He is currently working on its sequel. Also, another novel using magical realism is running around the back of his mind.

Jim Wilder blends his love of song writing and poems to create personal accounts of life. Most of his works have a comedic twist but he is capable of heart wrenching lyrics. Many of his pieces have been translated into Spanish and performed in Nicaragua.

Nathaniel Robert "Bob" Winters grew up in N.Y.C. The Navy Vietnam Veteran earned a BA from Sonoma State University and a Master's from CSU Stanislaus. The retired teacher lives with his wife/muse in the Napa Valley. Despite having Parkinson's disease, he writes every day. He has published 15 books in the last 10 years.

Jean Wong, an award winning poet, fiction, and writer of *Sleeping with the Gods* and *Hurtling Jade*, has had work produced by Petaluma, Off the Page, Lucky Penny Reader's Theater, and Sixth Street Playhouse. Jean writes from the bottom of a well, amazed to look up and see the sky.

Artists' Statements

Warren Bellows states "painting is my meditative and passionate way to inquire into the nature of reality. Besides exploring the natural world in landscapes, I visually play with ideas embedded in Quantum Physics, Chaos Theory and the Multiverse. I call upon my decades of experience as an acupuncturist to help me bring movement and vitality to my brushstrokes. Many hidden worlds often emerge from these energetic strokes.

This particular inquiry of mine should last for an eternity which hopefully means I will get to dance with Beauty for a very long time."

www.wbellows.com

Christine MacDonald's paintings often depict evocative encounters between wild creatures, or, between humans and creatures. She is particularly drawn to using images of ravens, crows and hares in her work. These creatures inhabited the landscapes of her childhood, growing up on the remote Hebridean island of Tiree, off the west coast of Scotland. The realization that they all share the distinction of being mythologized as otherworldly presences worldwide, and not only in Celtic folklore, came later.

Christine studied fine art at the University of Sussex, England, and graduated with a B.A. degree with honors, in painting. She maintains a studio near the town of Sonoma, where ravens and jackrabbits still share the land. Her sense of reverence for, and longing for, a wordless communication with nature (the Other) drives her work—sometimes poignantly, sometimes with humor.

www.christinemacdonald.com

Redwood Branch History

Jack London was first attracted to the beauty of Sonoma County in 1909, the very year he was named an honorary founding member of the Berkeley-based California Writers Club [CWC].

In 1975 Redwood Writers was established as the fourth CWC branch, due to special impetus from Helene S. Barnhart of the Berkeley Branch, who had relocated to the North Bay. She and forty-five charter members founded the Redwood Branch of the CWC.

Redwood Writers is a non-profit organization whose motto is: "writers helping writers." The organization's mission is to provide a friendly and inspirational environment in which members may meet, network, and learn about the writing industry.

Monthly meetings are open to the public and feature professional speakers who present a variety of topics from writing skills to publishing and marketing.

The club sponsors a variety of activities, such as Contests and Workshops. Every other year the club holds a day-long Writers Conference, offering seminars on all areas of writing.

Redwood Writers publishes a members' anthology, now celebrating thirteen consecutive years, in addition to a poetry anthology, giving members an opportunity to publish their work.

In cooperation with the county's largest bookstore, Copperfield's Books, Redwood Writers presents "Hot Summer Nights," where members' books are reviewed for discussion at meetings open to the general public. Each year, club members staff a booth at the Sonoma County Fair, where books are sold and writing tips are offered to Fair attendees.

An extensive monthly newsletter and award winning website, along with other social media outlets, keep members in touch with one another, to share accomplishments and successes.

Redwood Writers is indebted to its founders and charter members, to the leaders who have served at the helm, and to our many members. Without this volunteer dedication, Redwood Writers could not have developed into the professional club it is today with over 300 members. For more information visit *www.redwoodwriters.org.*

Redwood Writers Presidents

Redwood Branch is indebted to its founders, charter members, and to the leaders who have served at the helm, and, of course, to our many members. Without their volunteer hours and dedication to the club's mission, Redwood Writers could not have developed into the professional and successful club it is today with 300 members.

1975	Helen Schellenberg Barnhart	1992	Barb Truax (4 years)
1976	Dianne Kurlfinke	1997	Marvin Steinbock (2 years)
1977	Natlee Kenoyer	1999	Dorothy Molyneaux
1978	Inman Whipple	2000	Carol McConkie
1979	Herschel Cozine	2001	Gil Mansergh (2 years)
1980	Edward Dolan	2003	Carol McConkie
1981	Alla Crone Hayden	2004	Charles Brashear
1982	Mildred Fish	2005	Linda C. McCabe (2 years)
1983	Waldo Boyd	2007	Karen Batchelor (2 years)
1984	Margaret Scariano	2009	Linda Loveland Reid (3 years)
1985	Dave Arnold	2013	Robbi Sommers Bryant (1.5 years)
1986	Mary Priest (2 years)	2015	Sandy Baker (2 years)
1988	Marion McMurtry (2 years)	2017	Roger C. Lubeck (2 years)
1990	Mary Varley (2 years)		

Awards

Jack London Award

Every other year, CWC branches may nominate a member to receive the Jack London Award for outstanding service to the branch, sponsored by CWC Central. The recipients are:

1975	Helen Schellenberg Barnhart	1998	Barbara Truax
1977	Dianne Kurlfinke	2003	Nadenia Newkirk
1979	Peggy Ray	2004	Gil Mansergh
1981	Pat Patterson	2005	Mary Rosenthal
1983	Inman Whipple	2007	Catherine Keegan
1985	Ruth Irma Walker	2009	Karen Batchelor
1987	Margaret Scariano	2011	Linda C. McCabe
1989	Mary Priest	2013	Linda Loveland Reid
1991	Waldo Boyd	2015	Jeane Slone
1993	Alla Crone Hayden	2017	Sandy Baker
1995	Mildred Fish		
1997	Mary Varley		

Helene S. Barnhart Award

In 2010 this award was instituted, inspired by Redwood Writers first president, to honor outstanding service to the branch, given in alternate years to the Jack London Award.

2010	Kate (Catharine) Farrell	2016	Robin Moore
2012	Ana Manwaring	2018	Malena Eljumaily
2014	Juanita J. Martin		

Additional copies
of this book
may be purchased at
amazon.com
and other retail outlets.